Second Edition

LEARNING EXPERIENCES IN SPORT PSYCHOLOGY

Glyn C. Roberts, PhD
Norwegian University of Sport Science

Kevin S. Spink, PhD
University of Saskatchewan

Cynthia L. Pemberton, PhD
University of Missouri–Kansas City

Human Kinetics

Library of Congress Cataloging-in-Publication Data

Roberts, Glyn C.
    Learning experiences in sport psychology / by Glyn C. Roberts,
Kevin S. Spink, and Cynthia L. Pemberton. — 2nd ed.
      p. cm.
    Includes bibliographical references and index.
    ISBN 0-88011-932-2
    1. Sports—Psychological aspects.   2. Sports—Psychological
aspects—Research.   I. Spink, Kevin S., 1952-   II. Pemberton,
Cynthia L., 1956-   III. Title
  GV706.4.R63 1999
  796'.01—dc21   98-30815
                                            CIP

ISBN: 0-88011-932-2
Copyright © 1999 by Glyn C. Roberts and Kevin S. Spink

Acquisitions Editor: Steve Pope; **Developmental Editor:** Syd Slobodnik; **Managing Editor:** Katy Patterson; **Assistant Editor:** Leigh LaHood; **Copyeditor:** Denelle Eknes; **Proofreader:** Ann M. Bruehler; **Indexer:** Joan Griffitts; **Graphic Designer:** Nancy Rasmus; **Graphic Artist:** Tom Roberts; **Photo Editor:** Boyd LaFoon; **Cover Designer:** Keith Blomberg; **Illustrator:** Tom Roberts; **Printer:** United Graphics

Printed in the United States of America

10 9 8 7 6 5 4 3 2 1

Human Kinetics
Web site: http://www.humankinetics.com/

United States: Human Kinetics
P.O. Box 5076
Champaign, IL 61825-5076
1-800-747-4457
e-mail: humank@hkusa.com

Canada: Human Kinetics
475 Devonshire Road Unit 100
Windsor, ON N8Y 2L5
1-800-465-7301 (in Canada only)
e-mail: humank@hkcanada.com

Europe: Human Kinetics, P.O. Box IW14
Leeds LS16 6TR, United Kingdom
(44) 1132 781708
e-mail: humank@hkeurope.com

Australia: Human Kinetics
57A Price Avenue
Lower Mitcham, South Australia 5062
(088) 277 1555
e-mail: humank@hkaustralia.com

New Zealand: Human Kinetics
P.O. Box 105-231, Auckland 1
(09) 523 3462
e-mail: humank@hknewz.com

CONTENTS

PREFACE

The purpose of *Learning Experiences in Sport Psychology* is to develop an understanding of the scientific process when applied to sport psychology. The learning experiences we have devised are designed to help you ask relevant questions and to develop the skills necessary to answer these questions. Our discussion is limited to the psychology of sport, with some references to exercise psychology, but the procedures and skills apply to other social and behavioral sciences.

The learning experiences are representative of the skills and research strategies scientists need to address questions as they apply to sport psychology. Each learning experience introduces a psychological construct or process and addresses a question pertaining to that construct or process. Then one scientific strategy for answering that question is given. In this way, by the end of the course, you will have been introduced to several psychological phenomena as well as many research skills, procedures and strategies by which to further understand the phenomena. You will not only become relatively knowledgeable about the research process, but you also will be knowledgeable about many of the important psychological processes that affect individuals when they engage in sport environments.

This learning experience book is meant to complement lectures in the psychology of sport. It is not meant to be an exhaustive text in and of itself. Rather, it provides the hands-on experience so essential to fully understanding psychological processes as they operate in sport.

This book has been divided into three parts: Research Methods Experiences, Understanding Sport Psychological Phenomena, and Applying Sport Psychological Phenomena. Although each learning experience is an independent unit, you will find that each one follows a similar format. The general format is as follows:

1. An introduction to the phenomenon is given.
2. A list of objectives of the learning experience is given to anticipate major points under consideration.
3. The basic considerations of the phenomenon are given in which the literature on the topic is presented.
4. You are presented with a specific task or assignment designed to give you first-hand experience in examining and dealing with the psychological concept under discussion and are given a specific procedure to follow. This scientific procedure will be outlined, and you are to conduct the empirical study. You then present the data you have collected.
5. A class discussion will focus on questions concerned with the specific data you have collected and analyzed and with general issues in the topic area.

To understand the scientific concerns that all sport psychologists must address, the first segment of the book, Research Methods Experiences, introduces you to the major concepts every scientist in sport psychology must understand. In this section you will learn that it is important to ask appropriate scientific questions, be given general procedures by which questions may be answered, and be informed of some procedures to utilize in analyzing and presenting your data for evaluation by yourself and fellow sport scientists. Understanding this first section of the book is vital, for much of what follows assumes you know this material. Work through the first five learning experiences carefully.

The second section of the book, which looks at eight popular psychological processes, introduces you to the major research approaches of sport scientists. These experiences will help you to understand how the phenomena operate in sport settings and the ways that sport scientists go about attempting to gain a deeper understanding of them.

The third section of the book is a little different in that seven topics are chosen that pertain to the application of our knowledge to help athletes in sport settings. These learning experiences introduce you to the psychological skills and coaching strategies that may be used to assist athletes either to cope with the stresses of athletic participation or to enhance their own performance.

One benefit of understanding these psychological phenomena is that you may gain a better understanding of yourself when you perform in competitive sport settings. But, more than that, as a future teacher, coach, or parent, you will be more sensitive to the psychological processes that affect the behavior of athletes, or your own children. Through these experiences, you will develop both an understanding of the skills and strategies necessary to be an objective observer of psychological behavior in sport and an insight into and knowledge of the psychological processes that will make you a more mature, sensitive, and competent teacher, coach, or parent.

ACKNOWLEDGMENTS

When writing a learning experience workbook such as this, we inevitably use the skill and efforts of colleagues, both here and elsewhere. To all those colleagues who find their work represented here, we trust that you will not be too irritated with our brief overviews. However, we wish to acknowledge the excellent research conducted by our colleagues and thank them for their contributions. In particular, we wish to acknowledge our present and former colleagues, Drs. Susan Greendorfer, Maria Allison, and Linda Koehler, for their contributions to the original workbook we published in 1979 (Roberts, G.C., Allison, M.T., Greendorfer, S.L., Spink, K.S., & Koehler, L.S. 1979. *Social science of play games and sport: Learning experiences.* Champaign, IL: Human Kinetics). Even though the present workbook has changed much from the original, many of the initial ideas are the same.

This revision of the 1986 book (Roberts, G.C., Spink, K.S., & Pemberton, C.L. 1986. *Learning experiences in sport psychology.* Champaign, IL: Human Kinetics) was written by Kevin Spink and me. For personal reasons, Cindy Pemberton was unable to collaborate with us on this second edition in the time schedule we set for ourselves. She was sorely missed. Therefore, any blame for errors or misinterpretations should be directed at Kevin and me. But, because we retained much of what we co-authored in 1986, we have maintained Cindy's name as co-author. And if there is another revision in the future, Cindy will be an active collaborator once more. We missed you, Cindy!

We want to thank the many undergraduates, many who have not been shy in giving us their opinion on the experiences used in this book, for their constructive and not-so-constructive criticisms! We have tried to tailor many of the experiences to make them student-friendly. We also want to acknowledge the legion of graduate students who have been instructors in the course where we used these experiences. We have tried to incorporate many of the ideas and pedagogically sensitive suggestions they gave us.

PART I

RESEARCH METHODS EXPERIENCES

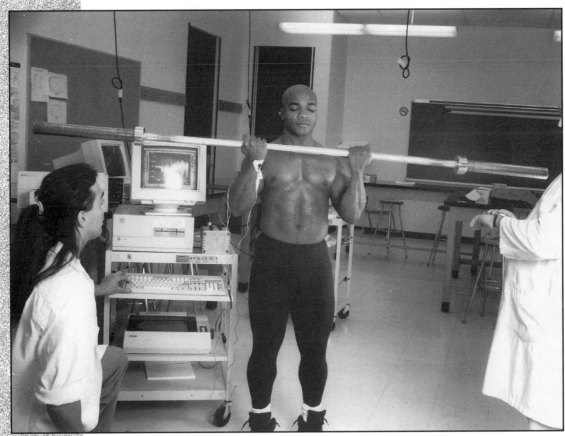

EXPERIENCE 1

ASKING THE RESEARCH QUESTION

Have you ever wondered why some athletes respond well to competitive pressure and others do not? Are you curious about whether women can be as psychologically competitive as men? Is Little League a beneficial experience for children? Do home teams really have a psychological advantage? Can athletes learn to cope with psychological pressure in important games? Many such questions come to mind to those who participate in or observe modern sport. We all have opinions on these matters, but the best way to answer them is to use the systematic procedures of the scientific method. The first step in the scientific method is to ask an appropriate question and develop testable hypotheses from that question. The purpose of experience 1 is to help you learn this step.

Objectives

In this learning experience you will learn how

- to ask a research question,
- to distinguish between an independent variable and a dependent variable, and
- to operationalize the research question.

Then you will have the opportunity to formulate your own research question and develop hypotheses from your question.

Basic Considerations

The purpose of the scientific method is to obtain clear answers to research questions. Rather than relying on opinion, hearsay, or isolated experiences, the researcher states a clear question, then determines a logical and systematic way to achieve an answer. The scientist is a curious person who asks a question and designs a study to answer it. Asking the question is the first step in the research process. It is also the

3

most crucial step, because the way the question is asked determines the direction of the research.

The research question should have these qualities. It should ask about the relationship between variables, be concise and specific, and be testable. A *variable* is any factor in whose change the researcher is interested. For example, the researcher may be interested in the effect of arousal on sport performance. The specific question may be, "Does high arousal facilitate sport performance?" In this example, arousal is a *psychological construct.* A psychological construct is a variable within the person, and it is these types of variables that are interesting to sport psychologists. In this case, both arousal and sport performance are subject to variation (changes) and are thereby termed variables. However, one is an *independent* variable and the other is a *dependent* variable.

The independent variable is the one the researcher is trying to understand. In the example, the independent variable is arousal. The researcher wants to understand the effect of arousal on sport performance. When arousal is high, does it facilitate the athlete's performance? The dependent variable is the consequent of the independent variable, and it is the variable measured to determine the effect of the independent variable. In the example, sport performance is the dependent variable to measure the effect of arousal. When arousal is high, does it facilitate the athlete's performance or interfere with it? To investigate the effects of arousal on performance, the researcher needs to measure sport performance while controlling levels of arousal.

To illustrate with a second example, another research question might be, "Is participation in Little League beneficial for children?" What are the independent variable and the dependent variable? In other words, which variable is the researcher trying to understand and which variable will he or she measure to investigate the effect? In this case, the independent variable is participation in Little League and the dependent measure is the benefit to the children. Thus, the nature of the relationship is as follows:

Participation in Little League   ⟶   Benefit to children
(independent variable)   (dependent variable)

In asking the research question and identifying the independent and dependent variables, the researcher assumes that the variables change in some systematic way. The research investigation sets out to capture that change. To do so, the researcher must reduce the research question to measurable units, that is, must *operationalize* the variables. When the researcher operationalizes the variables, he or she makes decisions on how to measure them.

For the question about participation in Little League, both variables are stated in general terms. How is the researcher to define participation and benefit in measurable units? Does participation mean continued participation over several years, or can the researcher use participants who have been competing for one year (or less)? Is the researcher interested in the competitive intensity of the various leagues, or does that not matter? Also, how is the researcher to measure benefit? Is the researcher interested in prosocial behavior, moral development, self-esteem, or some other measure of benefit? In other words, exactly how can we define sport participation in measurable terms, and how can we measure benefit so we can understand the effect of participation? These are important decisions that the researcher must make before beginning to answer the question.

For the question about the effect of arousal on sport performance, the researcher must go through the same process to operationalize the variables. How will he or she measure arousal? Does the researcher use heart rate recordings, a pencil-and-paper anxiety questionnaire, a measure of perspiration secretion, or some other measure? Also, how is sport performance to be operationalized? Does the researcher take one sport or several sports? Does he or she use easily recorded measures such as batting performance in baseball, points made in basketball, goals scored in hockey, and so on? Does he or she use team measures (like winning or losing) or individual measures? The researcher must resolve these and many more questions before being ready to answer the research question.

As the researcher resolves these questions, he or she defines the procedures to follow in answering the question. Further, decisions pertaining to the measurement technology of the investigation allow the researcher to make educated guesses about the findings of the study. The researcher is now ready to formulate the *hypotheses*.

Hypotheses are important tools in the research process and every study should have them. A hypothesis is a deduced statement (always in the present tense) that specifies the direction the data will take when the study is conducted. For example, regarding the effect of arousal on sport performance, a plausible hypothesis would be:

The higher the arousal, the higher the sport performance of athletes.

The hypothesis is the researcher's best guess (based on reading and thinking) at specifying the direction that he or she believes the data will go.

The hypothesis must also be sensitive to the decisions about how the researcher will operationalize the variables. Thus, the hypotheses specify the operationalization of the variables. In the example, the researcher might decide that heart rate is the measure of arousal and that baseball batting average is the measure of sport performance. He or she would then need to test the following specific hypotheses.

General question.   What is the effect of arousal on sport performance?

Hypothesis 1.   The higher the level of heart rate, the higher the level of batting performance.

Hypothesis 2.   The lower the level of heart rate, the lower the level of batting performance.

In this example, the hypotheses state that a linear (straight line) relationship exists between level of arousal and sport performance. As arousal increases, performance improves. However, is that what really happens? At this point the researcher is ready to move to the next stage of the investigation—the design.

Learning Experience

Purpose

- To develop the skill to ask a good research question.
- To develop the skill to deduce specific testable hypotheses from the general question.

Procedure

1. Following is a list of variables. Take any two variables and determine how they might logically be related.

Anxiety	Stress	Sport performance
Age	Reinforcement	Risk taking
Audience	Aggression	Prosocial behavior
Competition	Sport participation	Cheating

2. Write a general research question using the two variables you have chosen. For example, "Do different levels of anxiety affect the amount of aggression exhibited during competition?"

General research question _____

_____

3. Make a decision about how you plan to operationalize the independent and dependent variables.

Operationalization:

Independent variable _____

_____

Dependent variable _____

_____

4. Formulate hypotheses (at least two) that stem from the question. Make sure each hypothesis specifies a relationship between the two variables and uses the operationalized variables.

Hypothesis 1 _____

_____

Hypothesis 2 _____

_____

5. Develop your own specific question on any topic relevant to sport psychology. Remember, when you state your hypotheses, they have to be specific and measurable.

Discussion Questions

After you have developed a question and operationalized the variables, discuss the following questions and others you may have in class among your classmates and the instructor.

1. Why is it important to operationalize variables?

2. Why is it important to make sure that hypotheses are specific and testable?

3. Why is asking the question the most important step in the research process?

Suggested Reading

For further information, consult the following references:

Kerlinger, F. (1973). *Foundations of behavioral research.* New York: Holt, Rinehart & Winston.

Thomas, J., & Nelson, J. (1996). *Research methods in physical activity.* (3rd ed.) Champaign, IL: Human Kinetics.

EXPERIENCE 2

REVIEWING THE LITERATURE

The first and most important step in the research process is asking the question and deriving hypotheses. The question and hypotheses then dictate how the researcher tries to find an answer. The first step in finding the answer is to review the literature to determine what has been written on the topic.

Objectives

In this learning experience you will learn

- the purposes of a literature review, and
- how to begin a review of the literature.

Then you will have the opportunity to embark on a scavenger hunt for specific references in the library to develop a working knowledge of library sources. You will locate articles and write a short review of a topic of your choice.

Basic Considerations

The review of the literature has many purposes. First, it lets the researcher know what has been written on the topic. Other investigators may have asked the same question and deduced similar hypotheses. Indeed, when the researcher begins reading, he or she may find the answer to the question without conducting an investigation. So, the essential purpose of a literature review is to prevent researchers from replicating the investigation and reinventing the wheel.

Second, a review of the literature gives some insight into the nature of the question itself. Reading previous work on the topic allows the researcher to focus the question and hypotheses so he or she can conduct a better investigation. Furthermore, the review will suggest ways to find the answer. What procedures and investigative strategies have other researchers undertaken? The research methods of these studies will provide insight into what is most effective for the topic chosen. The researcher may decide, for example, to replicate a previous study with some minor modifications

9

or to reject an ineffective procedure for measuring a variable. By reviewing the literature, the researcher will be able to think more clearly about the topic and better design investigations to test his or her hypotheses. The process is illustrated in figure 2.1.

Third, a literature review allows the researcher to document the rationale for the investigation. One obligation a researcher has is to report the findings of any studies so future researchers can benefit from the experience. Thus, every research study has a section reviewing the previous literature. In the review section of the study, the researcher presents the foundations of his or her project: the purpose of the study, an overview of the research to date, a critique of the findings and research procedures, and the specific questions and hypotheses. This allows future researchers to follow the arguments and evaluate the procedures.

The length of a review depends on many factors. First, more has been written about some topics than about others. Second, the researcher must decide the breadth of the review. Will the discussion include methodological as well as conceptual issues? How narrow or broad should operational definitions of the variables be? Should the review include only those studies that pertain directly to the topic or also include literature that indirectly pertains?

To begin a literature review, the researcher determines the categories or concepts he or she will study. The researcher then reads earlier studies that have investigated the topic, identifying relevant studies by referring to data bases and journal indexes.

Here is a useful tip for the beginning researcher. Find the most recent article available on the topic; then trace the references listed at the end of that article. Using arousal as an example, you might first look up an article on the topic in the most recent issue of the *Journal of Sport & Exercise Psychology*. Next, trace the references. Read through the articles systematically to learn about the categories or concepts on arousal that you have decided to study. Once you do this, writing the review of literature is easy. Document the articles as they pertain to your topic and prepare a description of the findings related to what you wish to study.

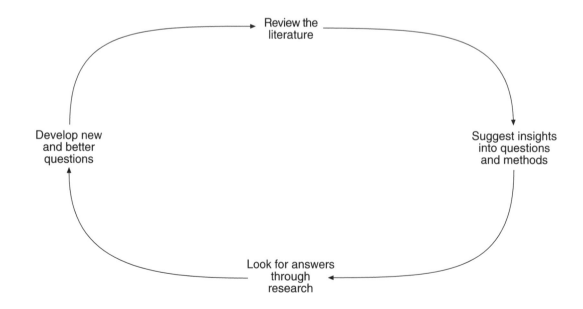

Figure 2.1   Process for gaining insight into the nature of the question.

Learning Experience

Purpose

- To develop a working knowledge of the varied sources and references available in your library.
- To focus a literature search on a specific topic and present a short review of the topic.

Procedure

There are many ways to become a knowledgeable user of the library. You can sign up for an introductory tour, read about how your library is organized, or ask the course instructor if he or she will give you an introductory tour. In particular, you should request information about where the following types of references are and how the library files pertinent information.

Dissertation Abstracts	Sport Bibliography (SIRC)	*Educational Abstracts*
Current research journals	SIRLS	*Current Contents*
Census data	*Psychological Abstracts*	SportSearch
Human resources area	Card catalogs for books and journals	

A useful experience is a literature scavenger hunt. Following you will find the titles of five articles on motivation in sport, with the names of the authors and the year published. Your first task is to find where these articles are published (specific journal, book, or dissertation) by searching logically through the references cited previously. Some will be much harder to find than others. This exercise will give you a feeling for how a library categorizes and organizes information. The second task is to complete the reference citation, with the name of the journal, or dissertation, or the publisher of the book.

1. Weinberg, R.S., & Gould D. (1995). *Foundations of sport and exercise psychology.*

_____

2. Roberts, G.C., & Treasure, D.C. (1992). *Children in sport.*

_____

3. Treasure, D.C. (1993). *A social-cognitive approach to understanding children's achievement behavior, cognitions, and affect in competitive sport.*

_____

4. Duda, J.L. (1992). *Motivation in sport settings: A goal perspective analysis.*

_____

5. Ames, C. (1987). *The enhancement of student motivation.*

_____

As an additional exercise, from the question you devised in the first learning experience, find five references pertaining to that topic. After you have identified and read the articles, write a brief literature review on your topic using these articles as your base.

Discussion Questions

1. What is the major advantage of doing a literature review?
2. What aspect of reviewing the literature gave you the most trouble? Do you know why?

Suggested Reading

For further information, consult the following reference:

Thomas, J., & Nelson, J. (1996). *Introduction to research in health, physical education, recreation, and dance.* Champaign, IL: Human Kinetics.

EXPERIENCE 3

ANSWERING THE RESEARCH QUESTION

Because collecting data is the basis of all science, every question the researcher asks requires a methodological approach appropriate to finding an answer. The methods you use are important considerations in the research process. In sport psychology, the five main categories of research methods for collecting data are the laboratory experiment, the field experiment, the field study, the survey, and the qualitative approach. As experience 1 demonstrated, the question the researcher asks dictates the methods to use in answering it. Each question requires a methodological approach appropriate for that particular question.

Objectives

In this learning experience you will learn

- the major considerations of any research project, including sampling, validity, reliability, and control;
- the five main categories of research methods; and
- the major data-gathering procedures, including behavior checklists, psychological inventories, interviews, questionnaires, qualitative methods, content analysis, sociometry, and using a research method dictated by the question asked.

Then you will have the opportunity to assess the appropriate method for the question and select a research design to answer it.

Basic Considerations

Before discussing specific methods of research and their procedures, we need to address two major issues: selecting the sample and determining the validity of the research technology you will use.

The Sample

One consideration that influences the method a researcher will use is the number of people (participants) who will participate in the study. The participants in the study are referred to as the *sample*. The sample should represent the total population the researcher is studying. To ensure that it does, everyone in the total population should have an equal chance of being selected at random for the study. The sample is then known as a *random sample*.

As an example, imagine a researcher wishes to measure anxiety in professional football players. To measure every professional football player (the *population*) is not possible or expedient; rather, the researcher seeks a representative sample. To achieve this, the researcher would select a sample from the population using some random procedure. The simplest random procedure is to put all the names in a receptacle (a hat!) and draw them one at a time until you get the desired sample number. Because all players have an equal chance of being selected, this is a random sample. The researcher then measures anxiety in those players selected.

As another example, a researcher wishes to survey the attitude of the townspeople toward a certain professional sport team. To obtain a representative sample, the researcher might use census data to pick names at random and send them an attitude survey. Because each person in town has an equal chance of being selected, the sample is random.

A random sampling procedure gives all members of the population an equal chance of being selected, but it is not always convenient, or practical, to randomly sample the total population. Other procedures then become appropriate. To sample university students, for example, it is not realistic to give each student in the United States an equal chance to participate. Thus, the researcher selects some universities at random and takes a sample from these universities. This procedure is known as *cluster sampling*.

A sport example of cluster sampling might be an investigation of psychological skills training on university or college varsity teams. It would be too time consuming and expensive for the researcher to sample all varsity teams. Thus, it becomes pragmatic to select those that are representative of the total population of varsity teams. The investigator could then sample athletes from these teams.

Another procedure for sampling is called *stratified random sampling*. A researcher may wish to sample subgroups within a population (e.g., black athletes). In this procedure the researcher samples from a naturally occurring group within a larger population. He or she selects one subgroup to compare with another subgroup. Thus, the researcher stratifies the sample (black athletes and nonblack athletes) and selects at random within the subgroups. This is a stratified random sample. The most common stratified random samples are drawn when researchers wish to study the impact of experience on athletes. A typical way to do this is to sample senior athletes on college teams and compare them with either freshmen or sophomores. The years are stratified; the athletes are chosen at random within the years.

The most important point is that the sample you research should represent the population you are testing. The only way to assume that the sample is representative is to adopt a random selection procedure. When the researcher does that, he or she can be confident that any findings represent the population.

Validity

The other important consideration in answering a research question is validity. The research method must allow the researcher to have a valid answer to the question.

To obtain a valid answer, the research must address two forms of validity—*internal validity* and *external validity*. Internal validity refers to the validity within the investigation; it is concerned with whether the study investigates what it is supposed to and whether it uses appropriate scientific methods. External validity refers to the extent to which the answer the researcher obtains may be generalized to the population at large.

To be internally valid, the study must measure what it is supposed to measure. If a researcher wishes to look at the performance differences between athletes who are high or low in anxiety, for example, then he or she must use a valid measure of anxiety. If the researcher uses personal knowledge of athletes to categorize them as high or low in anxiety, the validity of the procedure is questionable, because the researcher may focus on inappropriate cues or show biased interpretation toward friends. The research procedure should minimize the subjective interpretation of the researcher. (We will address the importance of objective and reliable measurement instruments later in the text.)

The researcher must be sensitive to all variables that affect the validity of the study. The fact that athletes know they are in a research study often affects their responses, in that some responses may be more socially desirable than others on a questionnaire. Moreover, athletes may be concerned that the coaches will read their responses. For these reasons and others, the researcher must guarantee confidentiality of responses so athletes answer as honestly as possible. (For a more detailed explanation of the factors that may affect the internal validity of a study, see Webb, Campbell, Schwartz, and Sechrest, 1966, which is a classic reference on these issues.)

External validity issues are closely tied to the adequacy of the sample. Generally, the more representative the sample, the more externally valid the study. External validity also refers to the adequacy of the research methods the researcher uses to answer the question. For example, much criticism has been leveled at laboratory experiments when the goal is understanding athletes in field environments. Laboratory experiments are sterile and artificial environments and, thus, inappropriate when the researcher is interested in athletes' behavior in the dynamic sport environment. This is one reason that field studies of sport contests have become more popular. We consider these studies more ecologically valid, as they are conducted in real-life settings. Certainly, they are more externally valid than laboratory experiments.

By considering the issues of sampling and validity, the neophyte researcher should be able to make intelligent choices about the appropriate methods to answer the question.

Methods of Research

The most important tool in science is valid and reliable data collection to verify hypotheses. Since the first (1979) and second (1986) editions of this book were published, a shift in emphasis has occurred in sport psychology. This shift is away from a heavy reliance on laboratory experiments toward a more balanced multimethod approach to gathering data, an approach that includes qualitative analyses. This edition reflects this shift. It also emphasizes that the five types of research methods we discuss are not mutually exclusive. The laboratory experiment, the field experiment, the field study, the survey, and qualitative methods all have their place in a comprehensive research program and we discuss each in turn.

Laboratory Experiment

The laboratory experiment gives the researcher the most control over variables and, thus, the highest internal validity. Because control of variables is the major benefit, and the effect of extraneous variables is accounted for, the researcher is confident that any observed differences are due to the construct under investigation. This is the major reason that psychology, and science in general, use laboratory experiments so frequently. In sport psychology, it has become popular to discredit laboratory experiments. The argument against laboratory experiments is that they are a far cry from the real world and lack ecological validity. However, the procedure can give us valuable insight into psychological processes.

In planning an experiment, the researcher must decide what relationship he or she wishes to demonstrate. The researcher then selects the procedures that allow the relationship to appear, if it exists. The researcher must always be aware that alternative interpretations might exist that explain the relationship. He or she must, therefore, design procedures that will eliminate or measure the degree to which extraneous variables affect the outcome. The way to do this is to include *control groups* in the experiment. A control group is a group of participants who are in the experiment but do not undergo the experimental procedures. The purpose of a control group is to clarify the nature of research variables and their relationships by comparing groups, those who undergo the effect of the variable compared with those who do not. This is an essential element in science.

An example might clarify this function. The question might be, "What is the effect of viewing violent sport films on subsequent aggressive behavior?" At first glance, it might seem appropriate to design an experiment in which one randomly chosen group viewed a violent sport film while another group, the control group, viewed a nonviolent sport film. However, the researcher must consider other possible influences on aggressive behavior. Could it be, for example, that aggression is the result of the arousal generated by viewing an exciting sport film and not simply the violence observed in the film? Other controls are necessary to answer this question.

To design an appropriate experiment so the researcher can be confident that any observed differences are due to the violent film, the researcher must include more than one control group. In this example, the researcher would have a group who viewed a violent sport film as an experimental condition. To control for any observed aggression that might be the function of the arousal generated by an exciting sport event, a control group of participants who watched an exciting, but nonviolent, sport film would be necessary. A second control group of participants who watched a nonexciting, nonviolent film would constitute the comparison group by which the researcher could assess the relative effect of viewing the films. By including the appropriate controls, the researcher can measure the relative effect of viewing violent sport films on aggressive behavior.

The laboratory experiment allows the researcher to isolate and manipulate the variable of interest. In this way, the researcher can understand the relative effect of this variable. For this reason, the laboratory experiment is a powerful tool for investigating psychological phenomena.

Although it is a powerful tool allowing the researcher to investigate variables of interest, the laboratory experiment depends on the expertise of the researcher to control for all relevant variables that may interact with the construct of interest. (This is where researchers demonstrate their competence to other scientists. The better researchers take most relevant variables into account in designing experiments.) Researchers can never be fully confident that all variables have been included, even though they design complex, multivariate experiments. Thus, although laboratory experiments provide meaningful insights into constructs, they cannot provide the entire answer to research questions. In the sport environment itself, variables not included in the experiment may impact the construct to radically affect behavior. In scientific terms, the researcher can be confident of the internal validity of the laboratory experiment, but never fully confident of the external validity.

It is for this reason that researchers in the sport sciences are advised not to rely on one research method. Rather, a multimethod procedure is recommended. Researchers should not only investigate variables in the laboratory but also determine their relative contributions with other research procedures. We want to enhance the ecological validity of our research.

Field Experiment

The second method of research, relatively ignored in sport psychology, is the field experiment. The field experiment is better than the laboratory experiment for collecting data because the study is conducted within as natural a setting as possible, enhancing external validity. The procedure is still an experiment, however, because the researcher attempts to control and manipulate variables. The field experiment may take two forms. In the first form, the investigator sets up the experiment in the sport or game environment and attempts to manipulate the independent variables. Although extremely difficult to conduct because the experimenter has much less control over the sport or game environment, the field experiment can provide valuable information.

As an example of a field experiment, let us briefly describe a study one of us did with a colleague (Kleiber & Roberts, 1981). We wished to investigate the effect of engagement in competitive sport (independent variable) on prosocial behavior (dependent variable). The prosocial behavior we chose in this context was a gift-giving task in which children were asked to share gift tokens with another child. To compare a competitive experience with a noncompetitive experience (the control group), the researchers provided a free-play environment where children engaged in their own games. An investigator observed the children to ensure that they did not engage in intensive competition. For the competitive sport experience, children played a kickball competitive game with adult coaches and umpires. In addition, to encourage the children to compete, many incentives were used, including trophy awards.

The children (sixth and seventh grade boys and girls) were randomly selected to the competitive group or the control group. The competitive-group children then engaged in a 2-week series of games in which the adults made the experience as competitive as possible. In doing so, the researchers manipulated the competitive environment of these children. The control-group children participated in their own (noncompetitive) games.

Results showed that the children in the competitive sport experience gave fewer gift tokens to other children than did children from the control group. Before we can conclude that the competitive sport experience is detrimental for all prosocial behavior, however, we must conduct additional studies using other measures of prosocial behavior. The important point here is that the researchers manipulated the independent variable and attempted to make the setting as realistic as possible to investigate participation in competitive games on prosocial behavior. Furthermore, the children were randomly selected into groups. The study, then, was an experiment within a field situation.

The second form of the field experiment takes advantage of a naturally occurring event and enhances the independent variables to test the construct of interest. In this case, although the researcher does manipulate the independent variable to some extent, he or she is not able to use complete randomization procedures. As an example, a researcher wishes to study the effect of a particular coaching strategy on the behaviors of players and selects an ongoing Little League competition. After obtaining permission to use the Little League competition, the researcher must decide which coaches will use the particular coaching strategy and which will be the control group. If the coaches agree to cooperate, the researcher may randomly choose which coaches will use the particular coaching style. Of course, the researcher does not randomly select the children to obtain data from. They belong to intact teams. Thus, the researcher does not have as much control in this situation as in the previous example.

Once the researcher has selected and carefully trained the coaches, he or she can begin the field experiment and, at the completion of the study, distribute question-naires to the players. The researcher then compares the responses of the players in the experimental group (the trained coaches) with the responses of the players in the control group to determine the effect of the coaching style. The design of this study is similar to the procedures Smith and Smoll and associates (1979) use in their ongoing investigations into coaching effectiveness.

In a field experiment, such as the Little League example, the researcher does not have complete control over the procedures. Many variables may influence the data to affect the results. Possible confounding variables include win-loss record, social climate of the team, or cohesiveness of the teams under study. If the researcher selects many teams, however, we may assume that these variables will affect the experimental and the control groups equally and, thus, not affect the overall results in a systematic way. For this reason, researchers include as many coaches as possible in such studies.

Either form of field experiment is desirable in sport psychology, because both forms are higher in external validity than laboratory experiments. They are difficult to conduct because of the high cooperation necessary from coaches and program administrators, which is not always possible to obtain. Researchers in sport psychology may resort to field studies for this reason.

Field Study

Field studies are increasing in sport psychology. They are useful because many behaviors of interest occur in natural settings that are difficult to replicate in the laboratory or in field experiments. The researcher uses the natural setting to study and analyze behavior but does not manipulate variables or arrange the environment. Because the events are occurring in their natural setting, the researcher must be careful not to intrude into the event itself. Any intrusion by the researcher affects the event, which may affect the observations.

The major task of the researcher, therefore, is to find a means to record observations unobtrusively. This is why researchers carefully develop and validate the measurement procedures. They do so in two ways, by *behavior checklists* or by *psychological testing instruments* used before, during, or after an event.

Behavior Checklist   A behavior checklist is a means of categorizing and recording behaviors of interest as they occur in an activity. The observer records the frequency or timing of certain behaviors. For example, in a professional football game, a researcher may be looking at incidents of prosocial behavior and whether winning or losing affects it. The researcher must determine what behaviors to record and how to record them. In this example, the researcher may record the number of times members of the opposing team help players up after tackles. Thus, prosocial behavior is defined as helping behavior. The researcher must decide how to record these incidents and other circumstances in which the behavior occurs, such as the score or the situation. Thus, the researcher must determine the behaviors and other circumstances to record to answer the question. The form of the final measuring instrument will depend on the purpose of the investigation. An example of a field study that uses a behavior checklist is given in experience 7, Social Reinforcement.

To develop a checklist, take the following steps:

Step 1.   Form a clear idea of the behavior you want to categorize. Is it a response to a stimulus, a behavioral act, or a measure of sport performance? In the previous example, the behavioral act designated as a measurement of prosocial behavior was helping a player of the opposing team up after a tackle.

Step 2.   Be sure that the unit of study is clear and specific so it cannot be misinterpreted. The behavioral act of helping a player after a tackle is unambiguous, but other behaviors often are more ambiguous. For example, if the response that interested the researcher was aggressive behavior, clear and specific measures would be difficult to obtain. Fighting is an obvious measure of aggressive behavior, but what about a robust late tackle of one player on another? Is it an act of aggressive behavior (an attempt to physically injure the opposing player) or is the act an unfortunate incident of overzealous play? To an observer, the interpretation is difficult. For this reason, researchers try to be as specific as possible in defining behaviors.

Step 3.   Decide how large a sample of the observed phenomenon you need to be representative. Should the researcher sample all behaviors during the entire game or take a random sample in each quarter? Should he or she wait for one team to score before recording acts or look only at losing teams? The researcher must make many similar decisions before the investigation can take place. Clearly, these decisions must be logical, depending on the purpose of the study. Then, the researcher sets up the checklist to record the appropriate observations.

Step 4.   Devise a method for recording the observations. The method should be simple and quick to use. If the observer must make decisions, then he or she must be highly trained so few errors occur. The more decisions you must make and the more complex the checklist, the greater the likelihood of errors creeping into the recording of observations.

Further, the researcher must make certain that the measuring procedure is as objective as possible. If the measuring procedure is mechanical (as in automatic timing of races), then no subjective bias will affect the results. Judgmental variables depend heavily on the subjective interpretation of the coders, however, so that coding error is always possible.

To assure the objectivity of judgments, the researcher must be concerned about the *reliability* of the measuring procedure. To be reliable, a measuring instrument should show similar scores of the same event on two separate occasions, and two separate people making measurements of the same event should have similar scores. To obtain reliability, the coders must always be well trained. The researcher is obligated to obtain a measure of reliability in any judgmental measuring procedure. The typical way to obtain reliable scores is to correlate the scores of two or more trained coders. This is termed interrater reliability. To be reliable, observers should obtain similar scores and the scores should correlate highly (.80 or better).

The researcher using a measuring instrument in the field is not content merely to establish reliability (as important as it is). The researcher also must be concerned with the *validity* of the judgments. A judgment is valid to the extent that it accurately reflects the intended construct. Is the checklist measuring what the researcher wants it to measure? The coders may be reliable, but they could be recording the wrong behaviors.

Establishing validity is a complex measurement issue. At best, the empirical procedures of testing for validity are indirect and inferential. Researchers use complex empirical procedures that allow them to determine convergent, discriminant, and predictive validity. For our purposes, we shall meet validity criteria by argument or logic, and this form of validity is called *face validity*. As a rule, using an instrument over time gives insight into the validity of the procedure. The researcher must always be aware of any limitations of the measurement procedures.

Psychological Measuring Instruments   The second form of measurement used in field studies is the psychological measuring instrument. Studies typically take an established measuring instrument and use it to gain insight into psychological phenomena. These studies also must be concerned with reliability and validity, but these issues usually have been resolved during the development of the instrument.

A researcher might use this measurement technique to determine the degree of competitive stress experienced by child athletes in various activities. The researcher has two major decisions to make: what measure of competitive stress to use and which activities to observe. The researcher should research the literature to determine if an appropriate measuring instrument exists. A likely decision of such a researcher would be to use the Competitive State Anxiety Inventory (CSAI-2) (Martens, Vealey, & Burton, 1990) to measure state anxiety, which is the anxiety you feel right now. This test was constructed specifically to measure perceived anxiety before or after a competitive environment. The second decision, concerning which activities to investigate, may involve team activities (e.g., baseball), individual activities (e.g., gymnastics), as well as nonsport competitive environments (e.g., band solos).

This is the project that Julie Simon (1977) conducted for her doctoral dissertation. Simon used the original CSAI (Martens, 1977) as a measure of competitive anxiety and tested children just before a competitive event to determine which activity generated the most anxiety. In her study, Simon found that band solos generated the most anxiety, followed by individual sports (wrestling and gymnastics); team sports were lowest.

A second example comes from the motivational literature. A researcher wishes to investigate the motivational determinants of achievement in sport. What are the psychological differences between those who seem to be high in motivation versus those who seem to be low? In this case, the researcher also has two major decisions to make: what measure of motivation to use and what criteria of achievement to adopt. The choice of instrument is more difficult because a decision will depend on the conceptual orientation of the researcher. A more traditional researcher, oriented toward personality traits, would use a motivational drive scale such as the Mehrabian measure of achieving tendency (Mehrabian, 1969). A cognitive-oriented researcher would probably use a contemporary, achievement goal orientation questionnaire, such as the Perception of Success Questionnaire (Roberts, Treasure, & Balague, 1998), which measures the degree of task and ego orientation (see learning experience 11, Understanding Motivation). The next decision is about the criteria of achievement. In a recent study by Roberts and Ommundsen (1996) for example, the authors selected the Perception of Success Questionnaire to determine whether athletes were ego or task oriented in goal orientation, and used questionnaires about the achievement strategies of the athletes in practice and in competition. They found that task-oriented athletes were more likely to seek coach approval and learn in practice than ego-oriented athletes. Ego-oriented athletes were more likely to avoid practice, preferring to compete instead.

The two examples show how researchers use field situations to gather data from players. They base the choice of instrument on the question they ask and the information they need to answer it. Thus, whether it is a recognized measuring instrument or an instrument constructed for the study, the researcher attempts to use the environmental dynamics of the sport contest to obtain data that are both reliable and valid.

Survey

If the researcher is not interested in using the sport setting to obtain information, but wants to obtain information about athletes (or any other population), the survey method becomes the most appropriate procedure. The survey is most useful for gathering information about the beliefs, attitudes, values, knowledge, and experiences of athletes. It is a useful first step in any research project, and its major benefit is to give a broad-based pool of information about the topic of study.

The survey is easy to administer and researchers can give it to many people in a short time. It is primarily a descriptive procedure and cannot be used to study cause-effect relationships. Thus, the investigator uses measures of association (e.g., correlations) to interpret the data gathered. These can be helpful in giving the researcher insights into sport phenomena.

Surveys take many forms, but the two most frequently used in sport psychology are the questionnaire (by mail or in person) and the interview (in person or on the telephone). The specific form is determined by the research question.

Survey Questionnaire   Because sport psychology is still a new area of study, researchers discover large gaps in the knowledge and understanding of athletes and athletic contexts. The gaps exist for elite and nonelite athletes, but particularly noticeable is the lack of information on female athletes and physically challenged athletes. Survey research is useful for gathering descriptive data to fill in the gaps before using other research procedures. Thus, as a first step in the research, survey questionnaires are useful tools.

Researchers use survey questionnaires to obtain two types of information. One is general-population characteristics such as attitudes, beliefs, cognitions, or experiences of athletes. Questions may focus on such topics as attitude toward sport issues or events, athletes' perceptions about sport occurrences, and athletes' beliefs about sport behavior. The second type of survey questionnaire concerns the nature and functioning of the team in the competitive environment. When the researcher is interested in the internal dynamics of the sport team, he or she asks questions that explore that function. For example, a researcher interested in the cohesiveness of the team might ask team members questions such as, "How cohesive do you feel the team to be?" "How close do you feel to your teammates?" To ask these questions, the researcher must construct a questionnaire.

Although it is often assumed that developing a questionnaire is a simple task, it takes a great deal of care to establish the reliability and validity of a survey questionnaire. A question worded one way has sometimes obtained a different response than the same question worded slightly differently. For example, a researcher may ask a question in such a way that athletes give the socially desirable response rather than a true response. The question, "When playing football, have you ever tried to deliberately injure someone?" would likely get fewer affirmative responses than the question, "When playing football, an emotional game, have you ever tried to deliberately injure someone in the heat of the moment?" The investigator must be careful to ask a question so the response reflects reality.

You can use many different formats to ask questions. The one the researcher selects will depend on the research question and how he or she intends to analyze the data. The three most popular formats for responses are scales, ranked lists, and checklists.

Scales. The most common scale in sport psychology is the *forced-choice scale.* As the name implies, the respondent is instructed to pick the one response that best describes his or her reaction and, thus, must make a choice. The most prevalent is the agree-disagree scale. The researcher makes a statement and requests that the respondent shows the degree of agreement or disagreement. The athlete circles the response that most clearly describes his or her feeling. An example follows:

Our team lost because we did not try hard.

1	2	3	4	5
Strongly agree	Agree	Uncertain	Disagree	Strongly disagree

In a variation of the agree-disagree scale, the researcher puts the extremes at either end of a continuum. Following is an example:

Our team won because we tried harder.

1	2	3	4	5	6	7	8	9
Strongly agree								Strongly disagree

The anchors of this scale are strongly agree and strongly disagree. The athlete determines where his or her feeling is best represented on the continuum. For analysis purposes, the two scales are not very different. With children, however, the first one is better because there is little to interpret. The child decides whether he or she agrees or disagrees, then decides how strong that feeling is. For adult athletes, the second scale is fine. In any case, the researcher must choose the appropriate scale.

Another form of scale popular in sport psychology is the frequency scale, which you can also use for behaviors or cognitions. The respondent circles the appropriate number, and this number is used in the analysis. Two examples follow:

When you participate in a contest, how often do you look at the official clock to see how much time is left?

1	2	3	4	5
Always	Frequently	Sometimes	Rarely	Never

Before I compete I am nervous.

1	**2**	**3**
Hardly ever	**Sometimes**	**Often**

Ranked list. Another form of questionnaire is a ranked list. The investigator asks the athlete to place items in order of importance. The ranks can then be totaled to determine the item of most importance for a group of athletes. The following example illustrates the format.

Rank the following elements in order of their importance in winning a game. Use the number 1 to indicate the element you think is the most important, number 2 the second most important, and so on until you have ranked each element.

_____**Individual game effort**

_____**Coaching**

_____**Teamwork**

_____**Team effort**

_____**Luck**

_____**Team ability**

Checklist. The checklist response is less useful than scales or ranked lists because it does not give degrees of response, and this information is sometimes important in sport psychology. The checklist response is not organized on any continuum or scale. The individual simply selects and checks the response that is true for him or her. This method is typically analyzed by calculating athletes' percent response in each category. An example follows:

When you play a sport, who is the person that most encourages you? Check one.

Coach

Teammates

Friends

Family

Other (specify)

Interview. The interview is becoming a frequently used tool in sport psychology, useful when the investigator wishes to probe deeply into beliefs, attitudes, cognitions, values, and other characteristics. One area in which the interview has been used effectively is ascertaining the reasons young children drop out of sport. Young children often have difficulty responding adequately to a questionnaire. The interview is therefore a useful procedure for these participants. For example, children typically respond that they drop out because the competitive sport experience "wasn't fun for me anymore." When asked why, they give the underlying reasons for their behavior, providing important data for sport psychologists. For any population that might have difficulty communicating in written form, the interview is a most useful tool. The interview is also useful if the researcher needs a deeper understanding of a phenomenon. For more detail on such interviews, see the following section on qualitative research. If the researcher is not looking at qualitative issues, but at more precise issues within sport psychology, then to be effective, he or she must structure an interview and train the interviewer well. The interviewer must know exactly what he or she is seeking and ask the same questions of everyone. If the interview is not structured (either face-to-face or on the telephone), the data are nearly impossible to use for comparison. Recording the interview and coding the data later is a good idea, because categorizing and coding the data is difficult to do during the interview. You can use scales and checklists to transfer the data obtained in interviews. A short interview is presented in a later learning experience.

Qualitative Research Methods

Without going into detail, we can characterize what we have described about research methodology in this section as *orthodox science*. This is the usual approach to pursuing knowledge. Up to now, we have embraced the normal scientific paradigm, as is evident in the acceptance of the rules and assumptions of normal science governing the pursuit of knowledge. One axiom of the orthodox view of science is that knowledge is gained through an objective process. It has been argued, however, that we can obtain knowledge in a subjective way, but its being subjective in character does not mean the knowledge gained is any less valuable. In an interesting and provocative article, Martens (1987) has argued that experiential knowledge is valuable and legitimate in sport and exercise psychology. The scientist becomes part of the knowledge process, and it is this experience and awareness that helps give meaning to the cues he or she is dealing with. In other words, the scientist has tacit knowledge, and this experiential knowledge gives meaning to the data. The researcher is part of the research process, and we must establish means to integrate this tacit knowledge into the process of understanding what is going on in sport and exercise.

What the new approach does is put the researcher in the center of the process of knowing. However, it also creates new ways of doing research to address the issue that the researcher is part of the process. Thus, the approach called qualitative research methods tries to recognize these realities. The approach also deals with many of the same issues as orthodox science, such as sampling, validity, and reliability of data, but it approaches them differently. Let us address these issues.

Sampling. In the orthodox science approach, we try to establish a random sample because we want to generalize to the population as a whole. The qualitative approach assumes that there are multiple realities, and generalizations to the population are not easy to make. Therefore, researchers using the qualitative approach want to obtain a *purposive* sample. Purposive sampling allows the researcher to select individuals who represent the needs of the research. For example, if you want to look at the rationale for coaching styles in youth sport programs, then it would be useful to seek coaches who represent apparently different styles. You would get a few coaches who represent the different styles, then interview them in depth to determine if any consistencies exist in the responses. This deliberate selecting of coaches is considered acceptable in the qualitative approach as they are a purposive sample who reflect the needs of the study and the researcher.

Reliability and validity. In the qualitative approach, we are not concerned with reliability and validity in the same way as we are in the orthodox science approach. We are still concerned with the same issue, but in this case we term it *trustworthiness* of the data. We want the data to be trustworthy. The concepts the qualitative researcher is concerned with are truth value, applicability, and consistency. To establish the credibility of the data, or truth value, we need to be certain that the data obtained from the individuals in the purposive sample accurately reflect what they meant to say. To do this, researchers use checks by giving the reported data to the individuals and asking them if this is an accurate reflection of what they said. In the example with the coaches, we would write the report from a coach who represented a certain style of coaching, show the report to the coach, and ask the coach if it accurately reflects his or her perceptions about coaching.

Even though researchers in the qualitative mold are not concerned with generalizability in the same way as the orthodox researcher, they are concerned with applicability of the data. For the researcher to accomplish this, he or she typically describes the context well. It is recognized that perceptions are context specific; therefore, describing the context allows other researchers to determine how applicable the research is to them. Consequently, qualitative researchers are concerned about describing in detail the situation from which they extracted the data.

Qualitative researchers are concerned about consistency, but in a different sense than the orthodox science approach. Orthodox science looks for stability and consistency, or reliability, over time, but the qualitative approach looks for consistency within context. For example, should a coach appear to be inconsistent in his coaching style from one day to the next, is it because he is inconsistent, or are there other factors that impact the choice of coaching style? Interviewing a coach who has just completed a session with senior elite athletes and interviewing the same coach a few days later, after coaching a youth sport contest, would probably produce different responses in terms of style. At least, one would hope so! So, the coach may be consistent within context. It is imperative that the researcher consider the total context as well as the process of coaching adopted.

Using an interview is the most popular procedure to collect data in the qualitative approach. However, researchers do not use the structured format of the orthodox researchers. Rather, they use an unstructured format in which the ordering and wording of the questions are left to the discretion of the interviewer. The researcher does not make a priori decisions about what is important, but lets the coach answer questions as he or she sees fit. The researcher may use questions as probes to elicit more detail, but is obliged to follow the thought processes of the participant rather than leading him or her through a series of questions. This process may seem cumbersome, but the researcher is more interested in capturing the reality as seen by the participant than on preordained assumptions. That is why the researcher is likely to record the interview. The researcher is more concerned with letting the participants follow their own thoughts on the question and making sense of them later. The researcher is likely to transcribe the data to written form so the participant can read the interpretation of the data by the researcher and correct or elaborate on meaning. This is a time-consuming procedure and can be costly in terms of recording and transcribing. However, once the data have been transcribed, the researcher then has to evaluate it and give it meaning. This is when researchers use their experiential knowledge to *content analyze* the data to render its meaning.

Content analysis. Using content analysis is a useful research in and of itself, as you can content analyze newspapers, magazines, books, and so on, as well as other forms of electronic communication (television, radio, movies). Content analysis is a method of systematically analyzing the content of any data source to determine the substance of the data. The tacit knowledge of the researcher is important to create categories for the data to give it meaning. In our previous example, the researcher groups the comments of the coaches into meaningful categories pertaining to the coaching style. In other words, we classify the information obtained through qualitative procedures. We could classify the comments around categories such as values, beliefs, contextual factors, and coaching behaviors, then subclassify within these categories. In that way, we begin to see the differences and similarities among the coaches and can build a picture of the determinants of coaching style.

Other Procedures

The methods that we have briefly discussed are not a comprehensive list. They are the methods used frequently by sport and exercise psychologists to investigate the issues of interest to them. Other procedures exist that are less frequently used. One method used by sport psychologists, based on *sociometry*, attempts to measure types of interpersonal relationships in a sport group. The relationship can be one of many, from friendship to leadership. The essential element of this procedure is that members of teams have to identify other members on the team based on the criterion of interest. For example, to investigate the leadership pattern of a team, a researcher might ask the question, "Which player on the team would you most like to have as the team captain?" After collecting the data, the researcher can illustrate the leadership dynamics through a diagrammatic representation. This can take the form of a table, a *sociomatrix*, or a dynamic representation called a *sociogram*.

To construct a sociomatrix of the leadership pattern of a basketball team, for example, the researcher asks each player on the 5-person team to choose one player to be captain. The researcher sets up a table with the names of the players listed along the side and across the top (see figure 3.1). The researcher enters a plus sign in the column that represents the choice of each player (e.g., Jack chose Jim). If 2 players choose each other (e.g., Jim and Doug), the researcher circles the plus sign to indicate a mutual choice. In this example, the totals indicate 2 isolates (Jack and John), 2 players who each receive 1 vote (Karl and Doug), and 1 player who receives 3 votes (Jim).

From the same data, we can create a sociogram by drawing lines of choice from one player to another. If players make mutual choices, we draw a line in each

	Jack	Jim	John	Karl	Doug
Jack		+			
Jim					⊕
John				+	
Karl		+			
Doug		⊕			
Total	0	3	0	1	1

Figure 3.1 Sample sociomatrix.

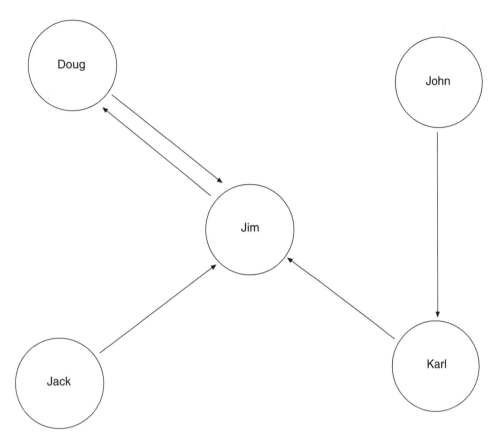

Figure 3.2 Sample sociogram.

direction (see figure 3.2). Thus, the sociogram indicates the dynamics of the leadership choices. The sociometric method is useful for exploring the nature of interpersonal relationships, and the construction of each sociomatrix and sociogram will depend on the question.

Learning Experience

Purpose

- To understand that the question determines the research method.
- To briefly design a research procedure to determine the accuracy of the research question.

Procedure

For each statement listed, describe the most appropriate research method for determining its accuracy. Be specific in your method and sampling procedures. For example, will you include a control group, and how will you select subjects?

1. Winning teams have lower state anxiety than losing teams.

   Research method _____

   Sampling procedure _____

   _____

   _____

   _____

   Probable research procedures _____

   _____

   _____

   _____

   _____

2. Highly anxious people do not perform motor skills as well as less anxious people.

   Research method _____

   Sampling procedure _____

   _____

   _____

   _____

   Probable research procedures _____

   _____

   _____

   _____

   _____

3. Men have more positive attitudes toward televised professional sports than women do.

   Research method _____

   Sampling procedure _____

   _____

   _____

   _____

   Probable research procedures _____

   _____

_____

_____

4. Children who engage in competitive sports are more aggressive in their social relationships than children who engage in free play.

    Research method _____

    Sampling procedure _____

        _____

        _____

        _____

    Probable research procedures _____

        _____

        _____

        _____

5. Women athletes have a better attitude toward women coaches than do men athletes.

    Research method _____

    Sampling procedure _____

        _____

        _____

        _____

    Probable research procedures _____

        _____

        _____

        _____

6. Sportswriters always write more about the winning team than the losing team.

    Research method _____

    Sampling procedure _____

        _____

        _____

        _____

    Probable research procedures _____

        _____

        _____

        _____

7. Youth sport coaches have different coaching ideologies than varsity sport coaches.

    Research method _____

    Sampling procedure _____

        _____

        _____

        _____

Probable research procedures   _____

_____

_____

_____

Discussion Questions

1. When you were choosing an approach to these statements, what was your primary criterion?
2. How did you address reliability and validity in selecting your research procedures?
3. What are the consequences of ignoring reliability and validity?
4. When designing studies, some scientists find it easier to design one type of study than another. For which statement was it easiest for you to design the study? Why do you think it was easiest?

References

Kleiber, D.A., & Roberts, G.C. (1981). The effects of sport experience in the development of social character: An exploratory investigation. *Journal of Sport Psychology, 3,* 114-122.

Martens, R. (1977). *Sport Competition Anxiety Test.* Champaign, IL: Human Kinetics.

Martens, R. (1987). Science, knowledge and sport psychology. *The Sport Psychologist, 1,* 29-55.

Martens, R., Vealey, R.S., & Burton, D. (1990). *Competitive anxiety in sport.* Champaign, IL: Human Kinetics.

Mehrabian, A. (1969). Measures of achieving tendency. *Education and Psychological Measurement, 29,* 445-451.

Roberts, G.C., & Ommundsen, Y. (1996). Effect of goal orientations on achievement beliefs, cognitions, and strategies in team sport. *Scandinavian Journal of Medicine and Science in Sport, 6,* 46-56.

Roberts, G.C., Treasure D.C., & Balague, G. (1998). Achievement goals in sport: The development and validation of the Perception of Success Questionnaire. *Journal of Sport Sciences, 19.*

Simon, J.A. (1977). *Children's anxiety in sport and non-sport evaluation activities.* Unpublished doctoral dissertation, University of Illinois, Urbana-Champaign.

Smith, R.E., Smoll, F.L., Hunt, E., Curtis, B., & Coppel, D.B. (1979). Psychology and the Bad News Bears. In G.C. Roberts and K.M. Newell (Eds.) *Psychology of motor behavior and sport.* Champaign, IL: Human Kinetics.

Webb, E.J., Campbell, D.T., Schwartz, R.D. & Sechrest, L. (1966). *Unobtrusive measures: Nonreactive research in the social sciences.* Chicago, IL: Rand McNally.

EXPERIENCE 4

ANALYZING AND PRESENTING DATA

Asking the question, reviewing the literature, deriving hypotheses, and designing the research methods for a study are the most difficult aspects in conducting research. Collecting the data, which will be the topic of the subsequent learning experiences, is the easiest and often the most enjoyable aspect. The task then is to make sense of the collected data. You must learn ways of analyzing data to interpret its significance and meaning to the question. Once you understand the meaning, you must learn ways to present the data to adequately and accurately summarize the findings.

Objectives

In this learning experience you will learn

- the difference between descriptive and inferential statistics,
- measures of central tendency,
- measures of variability,
- measures of association,
- the meaning of statistical significance, and
- methods of presenting your data.

Then you will have the opportunity to analyze and present a data set.

Basic Considerations

Analyzing Data

You can analyze and summarize the data that you have gathered by means of *descriptive statistics* or *inferential statistics*. Which one you use depends on the question. Briefly stated, descriptive statistics are ways for the researcher to summarize characteristics of the current sample. To report the attitudes or interests of a group of athletes about a topic, for example, the researcher would use descriptive statistics. Inferential statistics are much more complex and the researcher uses them to infer cause and effect relationships. To find the effect of psychological counseling on performance, for example, the researcher would design a study, with control group(s), and use the appropriate statistical analysis to see if a significant difference occurs between the groups. If a difference exists in the positive direction, the researcher would infer that counseling caused the effect.

Descriptive Statistics

Descriptive statistics are of three types. The first type deals with measures of *central tendency* (mean, median, mode); the second type deals with measures of *variability* (range, standard deviation, variance); and the third type deals with measures of *association* (correlation).

Measures of Central Tendency A basic assumption of science is that phenomena that occur in the natural world distribute themselves normally; that is, phenomena fall along a bell-shaped continuum called a *normal curve* (see figure 4.1). Most people fall in the middle, and as we go to each end of the continuum (low or high), fewer people are at these extremes. Sometimes people are distributed in greater numbers at one end or the other of a continuum, and this is called a skewed distribution. Typically, however, on most phenomena of interest to us in sport psychology, the constructs follow a normal distribution as illustrated in figure 4.1.

A useful statistic describing the sample is the *mean*. The mean is the average score. The statement that a basketball team has averaged 42 points in the second half, for example, is the same as saying that, over the season, the mean number of points scored in the second half is 42. The mean is computed by adding all scores on some measure and dividing by the number of cases (persons, games, and so forth). The mathematical formula for computing a mean is

$$\overline{X} = \frac{\Sigma X}{N}$$

where $\overline{X}$ = mean; X = raw score; Σ = sum of; ΣX = sum of all raw scores; and N = number of cases, participants, and so on.

As an example, if in 11 games a university basketball team scored the following points in the second half,

| 43 | 42 | 41 | 43 | 45 | 36 | 40 | 39 | 43 | 48 | 42 |

the mean would be the sum of the scores divided by the number of games:

$$\overline{X} = \frac{\Sigma X}{N}$$

$$\Sigma X = 462$$

$$\overline{X} = \frac{462}{11}$$

$$\overline{X} = 42$$

Two other useful measures of central tendency are the *median* and the *mode*.

The median is the single score that divides the set of scores in half. Thus, if the 11 scores in the example are rearranged from low to high so the distribution is as follows,

| 36 | 39 | 40 | 41 | 42 | 42 | 43 | 43 | 43 | 45 | 48 |

then the median is also 42. The median and the mean are not always equal, but it is true that the closer the median and the mean are, the more likely the distribution is normal. The mode is the number or score that occurs most frequently. In the example, the mode is 43.

Measures of Variability Although the mean is a useful statistic, it gives no idea of the spread of scores. This is where measures of variability are useful. The simplest measure of variability, the *range*, is the difference between the low score and the high score. A single score that is either high or low on a measure can dramatically alter the range (and consequently the mean). A more sensitive variability measure is a statistic called the *standard deviation*. This is calculated from the mean and represents the deviation or dispersion of scores around the mean. The standard deviation reflects the dispersion of scores in the following way (see figure 4.2). From one standard deviation above the mean to one standard deviation below the mean, approximately 68% of all scores fall. As shown in figure 4.2, approximately 13% of all scores are dispersed in the area from one standard deviation to two standard deviations above the mean and another 13% in the same area below the mean. The third standard deviation above and below the mean incorporates most of the rest of the scores. Thus, three standard deviations above and below the mean incorporate 99% of the scores in a normal curve.

The formula for calculating the standard deviation is as follows:

$$SD = \sqrt{\frac{\Sigma X^2 - \dfrac{(\Sigma X)^2}{N}}{N-1}}$$

where ΣX^2 = all raw scores squared individually, then added together; $(\Sigma X)^2$ = all raw scores first added together to calculate ΣX, then squared; and N = number of cases in the distribution.

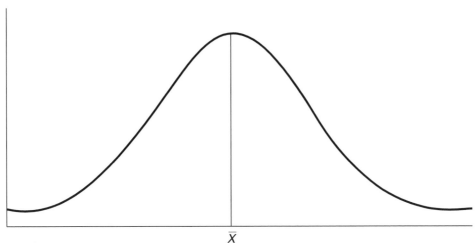

$\overline{X}$

Figure 4.1   Normal curve.

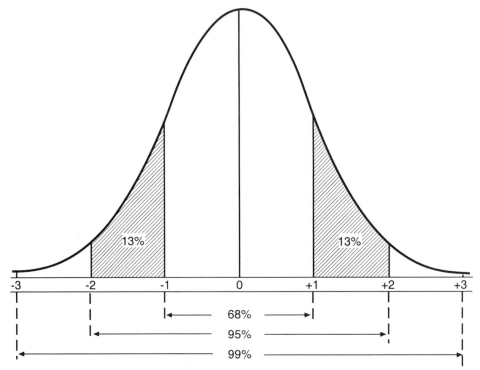

Figure 4.2 Normal curve with standard variations.

The standard deviation is much smaller than the range and is a more useful measure because the dispersal of scores from one standard deviation above and below the mean is known to encompass 68% of the scores. Thus, a small standard deviation means that the basketball team is consistent in the number of baskets scored in the second half. A large standard deviation, on the other hand, means that the basketball team varies considerably in the number of baskets scored in the second half. A coach should be concerned with a large standard deviation, as this may reflect a lack of motivation, teamwork, or other problems in the team.

You can calculate the standard deviation by substituting the basketball data reported on page 32 into the formula:

$$SD = \sqrt{\frac{\sum X^2 - \frac{\left(\sum X\right)^2}{N}}{N-1}}$$

$$SD = \sqrt{\frac{19502 - \frac{213444}{11}}{11-1}}$$

$$SD = \sqrt{\frac{19502 - 19404}{10}}$$

$$SD = \sqrt{\frac{98}{10}} = \sqrt{9.8} = \underline{3.1305}$$

The standard deviation of approximately 3 means that the team is consistent in the second half.

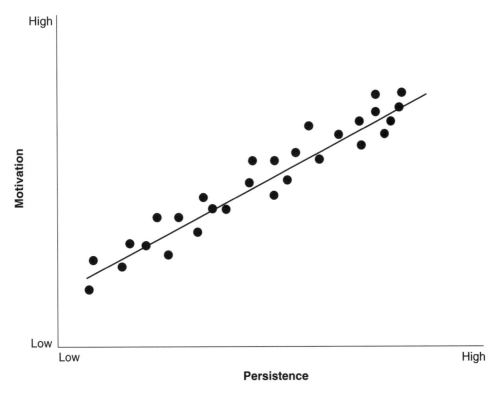

Figure 4.3   The association of motivation and persistence.

Another measure of the variability is the *variance*. The variance is directly linked to the standard deviation in that it is the standard deviation squared. It is thus computed in the same way as the standard deviation, except for stopping one step short; the square root is not obtained. The formula is as follows:

$$S^2 = \frac{\sum X^2 - \dfrac{(\sum X)^2}{N}}{N-1}$$

Although we will not include the variance in this series of learning experiences, it is a most useful statistic in complex analyses of data.

Measures of Association   The most commonly used descriptive statistic is a measure of association, or the relationship of one variable to another. The most used measure of association is the *correlation*. The degree of functional unity of one variable with another is measured with a correlation statistic. As an example, the researcher might be concerned with the degree of relationship between achievement motivation and persistence in a sport setting. He or she is concerned with the relationship of one variable (achievement motivation) with another (persistence). As is shown in figure 4.3, there seems to be a high relationship between achievement motivation and persistence. As motivation increases, so does persistence. A figure graphing the relationship does not give an objective measure of the relationship, however; for this, we must compute the correlation.

All correlations give a score that ranges from +1 to –1. A plus score indicates a positive relationship in that, as one variable increases, so does the other. The higher the correlation (i.e., the closer it is to +1 or –1), the greater the relationship. A score of +.96, for example, indicates a strong positive relationship. A score of –.96

indicates an equally strong relationship but in the opposite direction; that is, as one variable increases, the other variable decreases. A zero correlation means that the data are not associated (i.e., have no relationship) to each other in any systematic way.

Using correlations is a common procedure in science. The most common usage in sport psychology is in field studies, especially in determining the credibility of measuring instruments in field situations. Determining the objectivity, reliability, and validity (or trustworthiness) of a measuring instrument is an important step in science. If researchers do not have confidence in their measuring instruments, they cannot have confidence in the results of the study. The means by which they establish confidence are through correlational computations.

As an example, imagine that a researcher wishes to develop a forced-choice scale to measure the arousal individuals perceive in competitive sport environments. To determine the validity of the scale, he or she would need to correlate the scale with a known valid measure. For example, palmar sweat secretion is a valid indicator of arousal. Thus, it would be reasonable to correlate the pencil and paper scale being developed with the more cumbersome palmar sweat measuring procedures. If the correlation is high and positive (+.80 or above), the researcher can have confidence that the pencil and paper forced-choice scale is valid. But is it reliable and objective? To determine reliability, the researcher would administer the scale twice in similar situations (test-retest) and expect to find a high, positive correlation between the two administrations. Similarly, if two testers administer the same test in identical situations, the test is objective if the correlation is high and positive.

We can use many different correlations. Using one form rather than another depends on the data and the question. The most commonly used procedure is the Pearson product-moment correlation coefficient. In the example, we must determine the relationship between a sweat response measure and a pencil and paper anxiety score. The sweat response measure is a known valid measure of arousal, and it is necessary to determine whether the easier-to-administer pencil and paper measure approximates the sweat response measure. This is an accepted procedure to determine the construct validity of new measures. For each player there are two scores, the anxiety measure and the sweat measure. To determine the relationship, we follow the correlation procedures.

The correlation is always given the symbol r. The formula for the Pearson procedure is as follows:

$$r = \frac{\Sigma xy}{\sqrt{(\Sigma x^2)(\Sigma y^2)}}$$

where r = the correlation coefficient; x = the deviation of each X score from the group mean $\bar{X}$; y = the deviation of each Y score from the group mean $\bar{Y}$; Σx^2 = each x deviation score is squared, then summed; Σy^2 = each y deviation score is squared, then summed; and Σxy = each x score is multiplied by its corresponding y score, then summed.

The steps necessary to compute r are as follows (see table 4.1).

Step 1. Compute the mean for each set of scores.

Step 2. Subtract the appropriate mean from each raw score to obtain deviations from the mean. Place these deviation scores into two columns, one for each set of scores, as in table 4.1. These are the x and y scores.

Step 3. Square each x and y deviation score and sum them to form Σx^2 and Σy^2.

Table 4.1 Pearson Correlation Computation Example

	Test 1	Test 2	Deviations				
Player	Sweat score	SCAT	x	y	x^2	y^2	xy
1	8	26	3	6	9	36	18
2	9	28	4	8	16	64	32
3	4	20	−1	0	1	0	0
4	1	12	−4	−8	16	64	32
5	4	18	−1	−2	1	4	2
6	3	14	−2	−6	4	36	12
7	8	26	3	6	9	36	18
8	6	24	1	4	1	16	4
9	2	15	−3	−5	9	25	15
10	5	17	0	−3	0	9	0

$N=10$ $\Sigma X=50$ $\Sigma Y=200$ $\Sigma x^2=66$ $\Sigma y^2=290$ $\Sigma xy=133$

$\overline{X}=5.0$ $\overline{Y}=20.0$

$$r= \frac{\Sigma xy}{\sqrt{(\Sigma x^2)(\Sigma y^2)}}$$

$r = .96$ (high positive correlation)

Step 4. Multiply each x deviation score with its corresponding y deviation score to generate xy scores. Sum these scores to generate Σxy.

Step 5. Substitute these values in the formula to determine the correlation coefficient.

The example indicates that there is a high positive relationship between the test of anxiety and the measure of sweat response. This correlation allows the researcher to be confident in stating that the anxiety measure is a valid measure of arousal. This measure gives the degree of relationship, but it does not permit any statement about cause and effect. To determine cause and effect in science, we must use inferential statistics.

Inferential Statistics

Inferential statistics allow the researcher to mathematically determine the degree to which he or she can infer that characteristics from a sample can be generalized to a larger, broader population. Although we do much of this through sampling procedures, we must determine the probability that a sample is representative. The researcher sets up an investigation employing a statistical procedure to determine whether a variable caused a particular effect. With these mathematical procedures, the researcher determines if there is statistical significance (difference) between the means of two or more groups. If a statistical significance exists, he or she can be confident that the treatment, or the event being investigated, caused the difference and can be generalized to a larger population. If the results are not statistically significant, then any observed differences between groups are due to chance.

Statistical significance must not be confused with conceptual significance. A finding may be statistically nonsignificant, but the conceptual significance may be profound. If two different coaching styles made no statistical difference in the performance of teams, for example, this is an important finding in that it shows that we need give no concern to these particular coaching styles when focusing on team performance. This does not mean that coaching style may not affect other variables.

There are many mathematical techniques to test significance. The number of groups being studied and the number of variables under consideration determine the technique you will use. There are statistical solutions for multiple variables, but we will limit the discussion here to investigating the procedure that involves one dependent variable at a time to determine the significance between two groups. The particular procedure for the inference is called the t-test.

We use the t-test to determine if a significant difference exists between the means of two groups. As an example, to determine whether one of two different ways of teaching a motor skill is better, we must determine whether the observed difference in the means between the two groups was statistically significant. The t-test provides a mathematical solution. The data we use to determine significance are means and variances. By substituting mean scores and variances in the formula for t, we can determine its value.

$$ t = \frac{\overline{X}_1 - \overline{X}_2}{\sqrt{\dfrac{S_1^{\,2}}{N_1} + \dfrac{S_2^{\,2}}{N_2}}} $$

where t = value by which we will judge statistical significance, $\overline{X}_1$ = mean of group 1, $\overline{X}_2$ = mean of group 2, $S_1^{\,2}$ = the variance of group 1, $S_2^{\,2}$ = the variance of group 2, N_1 = the number of subjects in group 1, and N_2 = the number of subjects in group 2. As the formula shows, the size of t will vary depending on the variance and the size of the groups involved.

In a general sense, the larger the derived t-score, the more likely that the difference between the means is statistically significant. To determine whether the t-score is significant, we can use a table that gives various scores based on the degrees of freedom. Degrees of freedom refer to the total number of subjects in the investigation minus the number of groups in the study. The abbreviated table 4.2 indicates the values that must be reached for significance to be achieved. The complete table (table 4.5) is on page 43.

If the calculated t-score is equal to or exceeds the t-value in the table, then the means of the groups are statistically significant. For example, the researcher has 12 participants and 2 groups and derives a calculated t-score of 2.23; the degrees of freedom are 12 minus 2 (the number of groups), which equals 10. To be significant with 10 degrees of freedom the score must be equal to or greater than the table t-value. In this case, the result indicates that the difference between the 2 groups is significant at the .05 level ($p < .05$). This means that by chance the difference between the two groups would occur only 5 times out of 100. Thus, the probability is 95% that the differences between the 2 group means is a real difference.

Whenever you conduct a study, it is important to determine, before the study begins, the level of probability that you will accept for significance. The custom in sport psychology is either the .05 level or the .01 level of significance. Obviously, the .01 level is more conservative and means that if statistical significance is found at that level, the likelihood of the mean differences occurring by chance is only 1 in

100. The .01 level gives more confidence that the differences between means are real differences and not due to sampling error.

Methods of Presenting Data

It is sometimes useful to represent data graphically to give the investigator a better feel for the data. Thus, each researcher should devise ways to illustrate the results of an investigation. Researchers typically use means, totals, and percentages to construct figures, graphs, or tables. We give several examples here, but it is important to follow specific rules in constructing illustrations:

- Keep illustrations simple; do not overload or clutter them with irrelevant information.
- Label and mark them clearly; include a legend (description of symbols) when appropriate.
- Be sure that the units or levels you use in each illustration are consistent so that you can make true comparisons.

Figures

The most common figure used in sport psychology is the frequency polygon. Usually, researchers illustrate a data set using means for data points, which they connect with lines. The benefit is that differences between means are clearly emphasized as shown in figure 4.4.

To illustrate, data are represented along two axes. The horizontal line is referred to as the x axis, and the independent variable is usually placed along this axis. In figure 4.4, this is represented by environment. The vertical line is referred to as the y axis, and the dependent variable is usually reflected along this axis. In figure 4.4, this is represented by anxiety.

Another figure used in sport psychology, although less frequently, is the histogram, or bar graph. In this case, the bars represent the data. The independent and dependent variables are placed along the x axis and the y axis, respectively. The amount of sport encouragement given to boys and girls by family members, for example, might be graphed as shown in figure 4.5.

Table 4.2   Abbreviated Table of *t*-values at the .05 and .01 Levels of Probability

Degrees of freedom	*t* at .05	*t* at .01
1	12.706	63.657
2	4.303	9.925
3	3.182	5.841
5	2.571	4.032
10	2.228	3.169
40	2.021	2.704
120	1.980	2.617

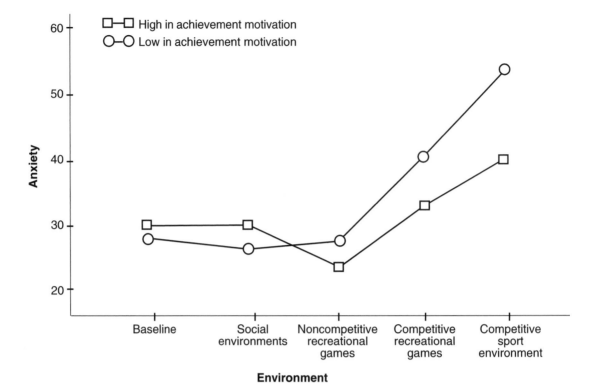

Figure 4.4 Situational anxiety perceived by athletes high and low in achievement motivation.

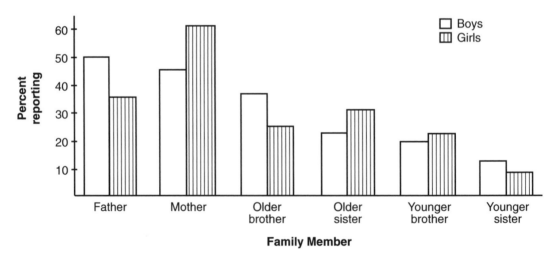

Figure 4.5 Sport encouragement given boys and girls by family members.

Other ways of illustrating data with figures exist, and the instructor will introduce them as necessary in the ensuing learning experiences.

Tables

Tables are like figures. They provide a great deal of data as succinctly as possible. The format depends on the nature of the data. To illustrate the appropriate use of tables, tables 4.3 and 4.4 were taken from two different studies in the literature.

Table 4.3   Basal, Observed and Adjusted Means and Standard Deviations for all Activities in the Precompetitive A-State Covariance Analysis

Activity	n	Basal A-state M	Basal A-state SD	Precompetitive A-state Observed M	Precompetitive A-state SD	Precompetitive A-state Adjusted M
Physical education	76	15.83	2.77	14.99	3.01	14.47
Football	181	14.56	2.49	15.59	3.03	15.77
Hockey	41	14.34	2.61	15.71	3.80	16.01
Baseball	51	14.35	1.87	15.92	3.81	16.22
Test	56	15.09	2.94	16.48	3.66	16.37
Swimming	56	15.07	2.70	17.07	3.08	16.97
Basketball	52	15.19	2.26	17.65	3.64	17.49
Band groups	105	15.47	2.30	18.28	3.98	17.96
Gymnastics	16	13.38	2.00	17.69	3.57	18.52
Wrestling	44	14.48	2.46	19.09	3.90	19.32
Band solos	26	14.31	2.46	21.15	3.52	21.48

Reprinted by permission from J.A. Simon. *Children's anxiety in sport and nonsport evaluative activities.* (Ph.D. diss, University of Illinois, 1977).

Table 4.4   Means and Standard Deviations for Trait Anxiety Scores

Treatment groups	M	SD
Low anxiety, low stress	30.39	3.40
Low anxiety, high stress	32.70	2.79
High anxiety, low stress	41.50	3.06
High anxiety, high stress	43.79	4.02

Learning Experience

Purpose

- To develop the ability to analyze and present data.
- To calculate the statistical significance of a set of data.

Procedure

The following sets of scores represent the amount of anxiety felt by experienced and inexperienced athletes before a sport contest. (A score of 1 represents a low level of anxiety, whereas a score of 10 represents a high level of anxiety.) Calculate the mean scores for each group. Choose a method to illustrate the scores. Finally, determine whether the means of the two groups are significantly different from each other.

Inexperienced athletes (group 1)		Experienced athletes (group 2)	
Subject no.	Score	Subject no.	Score
1	6	11	3
2	9	12	5
3	7	13	6
4	5	14	2
5	8	15	3
6	7	16	5
7	6	17	4
8	6	18	3
9	6	19	7
10	9	20	4
$\bar{X}_1 =$		$\bar{X}_2 =$	

Discussion Questions

1. Are the means of the two groups significantly different?
2. What method of illustrating the data did you choose? Why?
3. What is the standard deviation of the data? What does this tell you about the dispersal of scores?

Table 4.5   Table of *t*-values

Degrees of freedom	*t*-statistic (.05)
1	12.706
2	4.303
3	3.182
4	2.776
5	2.571
6	2.447
7	2.365
8	2.306
9	2.262
10	2.228
11	2.201
12	2.179
13	2.160
14	2.145
15	2.131
16	2.120
17	2.110
18	2.101
19	2.093
20	2.086
∞	1.960

Note. If calculated *t* is equal to or higher than *t*-value in the table, then difference is significant. If calculated *t* is lower than *t*-value in the table, then difference is not significant.

EXPERIENCE 5

THE FINAL PRODUCT

The four preceding learning experiences have presented the sequential order to follow in answering the original research question. As in any other educational endeavor, you must write up the project and share it with others. Research manuscripts require a particular format, although some flexibility is possible, depending on the scope and nature of the study. The major segments of a research article are the abstract, the introduction, the method, the results, the discussion, and the list of references. Though most articles will have these segments, not all of them are easy to read! However, it is not hard to set up a research report so that it is easy to follow. The purpose of this learning experience is to provide you with some basic elements of writing a research paper or report.

Objectives

In this learning experience you will learn

- how to organize a research report into the segments mentioned,
- what to include in an introduction,
- what to include in the methods section,
- how to report the results of your research,
- how to discuss the findings and relate them to previous research,
- what the reference format is for the articles used in your research, and
- what the issues are in scientific ethics.

Then you will have an opportunity to review a research article.

Basic Considerations

Writing the Research Report

An essential task for the sport psychologist is to share findings with the rest of the sport psychology community. We have an obligation to share our results so our peers and colleagues can assess and digest them. Typically, we share these findings through two avenues. First, there are scientific meetings where we report our latest findings and ideas, and we get instant feedback from our peers who are present. These meetings are arranged through professional societies, such as the North American Society for the Psychology of Sport and Physical Activity (NASPSPA) or the Association for the Advancement of Applied Sport Psychology (AAASP). We also have Division 47 (Sport Psychology) of the American Psychological Association (APA). These groups meet once a year somewhere in the United States (or sometimes Canada). They have keynote speakers who discuss their research avenues in detail; symposia where several people discuss a topic from different viewpoints; and individual research reports, which are either short oral presentations of 10 to 15 minutes or poster reports. These meetings are important for sport psychologists to remain up to date with the latest research findings and practice issues. There are also international meetings, where scientists from across the world get together to share findings. The best known for sport psychologists are the International Society of Sport Psychology (ISSP), which has its World Congress every four years somewhere in the world. The last four were held in Copenhagen, Denmark (1985); Singapore (1989); Lisbon, Portugal (1993); and Netanya, Israel (1997).

The second avenue of sharing information is the most important: publishing in research journals. It is also difficult and is getting increasingly difficult as the field of sport psychology grows. There are now more people in the field. In 1975, there were only about 250 people who were members of the professional associations in the United States. Now there are at least 1000 people who are registered members in the three professional associations in the United States. Many of these people try to publish their research in the major journals. As you can appreciate, the competition is severe. The best known journals to publish in for sport and exercise psychologists are *Journal of Sport & Exercise Psychology, International Journal of Sport Psychology, Journal of Applied Sport Psychology, The Sport Psychologist, Research Quarterly for Exercise and Sport,* and *Journal of Sport Behavior.* Each journal has its unique presentation style, but they all operate according to the *Publication Manual of the American Psychological Association (APA)* (4th ed.). It is the style we use throughout *Learning Experiences in Sport Psychology.*

As stated previously, research articles and reports usually have six segments: an abstract (about 150–200 words), an introduction where we review the past research, the methodology where we let our colleagues know how we conducted the study, the results where we report our findings, a discussion of the findings, and a list of all the research studies that we referenced in the body of the narrative. Let us look at each segment.

Abstract

The abstract summarizes the study, especially the question asked, the method, and a brief account of the findings. The abstract is an important part of the research report, as it is the first segment most researchers read to determine whether they wish to read the whole article.

Introduction

The introduction provides the reader with a review of the literature and a discussion of the problem we will deal with. Emphasize the importance of the topic in the introduction. The literature review, which places the research question into perspective, should include all relevant materials to provide a background for the work done to date on the topic. The introduction usually begins with the general problem and moves to the specific research question the study asks. It also defines the key terms and gives conceptual definition to the variables, both dependent and independent.

The length of the introduction will vary depending on the amount of relevant material available. As a rule, keep introductions short and relevant. What often makes an introduction long is developing theoretical arguments. The best research is anchored in theory, but try to avoid overlong statements. For a long introduction, we advise having subheadings for each key variable or concept. This will make it much easier for the reader to follow. The introduction should always end with a statement of the specific problem or question you will address in the study and the specific hypotheses. As an example, a statement used frequently to conclude an introduction section is, "The purpose of this study is to examine the nature of . . . ." It is advisable to state the specific research question, regardless of how you organize the introduction.

Method

The method section is the recipe for conducting the study. It first lists all the ingredients of the study, then gives the procedure for putting them together. The method section should be clear and inclusive, providing sufficient detail to enable anyone to replicate the study who wishes to do so. The section should include a description of the sample, the operational definitions of the dependent and independent variables, and the exact procedure followed in conducting the study. It is desirable to include the procedure by which you will analyze the data.

Results

The results section contains a description of the types of analyses you used and the results of these analyses as they pertain to the hypotheses of the study. It also includes all illustrations that are necessary to clearly represent data to readers.

Discussion

The most important section of a research paper is the discussion. Here the researcher discusses the general findings of the study and whether the findings support the previous literature on the topic. The researcher interprets the meaning of the study's findings and their relevance to the topic by comparing the results with previous studies in the area and with the hypotheses stated in the introduction. In addition, the researcher can give an opinion or speculation on the topic, and how the findings may have practical use for coaches, teachers, parents, and so on. The investigator may also discuss ways to conduct future studies to better address the question.

References

The final section of a research paper is a list of references. This section includes all the books, articles, and other sources that you have used in the study. The most widely accepted form of citing references is based on the *Publication Manual of the American Psychological Association* (4th ed.). All research libraries have copies of the manual. Some examples of the APA reference style follow:

- Journal article, single author: Gill, D.L. (1980). Success-failure attribu tions in competitive groups: An exception to egocentrism. *Journal of Sport Psychology, 2,* 106-114.
- Journal article, multiple authors: Gould, D., Horn, T., & Spreeman, J. (1983). Competitive anxiety in junior elite wrestlers. *Journal of Sport Psychology, 5,* 58-71.
- Edited book, multiple authors: Magill, R.A., Ash, M.J., & Smoll, F.L. (Eds.). (1982). *Children in sport—A contemporary anthology* (2nd ed.). Champaign, IL: Human Kinetics.
- Book, multiple authors: Vanek, M., & Cratty, B.J. (1970). *Psychology and the superior athlete.* New York: Macmillan.
- Article in an edited book: Martens, R. (1979). From smocks to jocks: A new adventure for sport psychologists. In P. Klavora & J. Daniels (Eds.), *Coach, athlete and the sport psychologist* (pp. 56-62). Champaign, IL: Human Kinetics.
- Unpublished manuscript: Lowe, C.A., Rejeski, W.J., & Green, S. (1981). *Non verbal expressiveness in attributions for performance on physical and intellectual tasks.* Unpublished manuscript, University of Connecticut, Storrs.
- Magazine article: Suinn, R.M. (1976, July). Body thinking: Psychology for Olympic champs. *Psychology Today,* pp. 38-43.
- Paper presented at a conference: Fisher, A.C. (1977, October). *Psychological analysis of sport activities from an individual differences perspective.* Paper presented at the Fourth World Congress of the International Society of Sport Psychology, Prague.

Cite every item in the reference list in the body of the manuscript and vice versa. Organize the reference list in alphabetical order.

Ethics of Scientific Investigation

A growing issue in science is every investigator's obligation to conduct the most ethical research studies possible and have respect for participants in research studies. As a researcher, one should have a definitive set of moral imperatives. We have two major categories of concern and we need to address both in our quest for ethical behavior. They are respect for humans participating in research studies and respect for the intellectual property of others.

Respect for Human Subjects

Every university has a policy governing the use of human subjects in behavioral research. In particular, these policies ensure that the rights of individuals in research projects are protected. These policies have been mandated by federal law. In studying the nature of human behavior in sport, most investigations obviously rely on people for information and answers to questions. The research must always protect the rights of these individuals by conducting research in a responsible and ethical way. The most important ethical considerations follow.

The Right to Refuse The participation of individuals is always voluntary. If a participant wishes not to participate for any reason, it is imperative that the researcher not force participation or jeopardize the rights of that participant in any way. A participant can refuse to continue with the procedure at any time during the study. Also, we must remember, parents have the right to refuse to allow their children to participate even if the child agrees.

The Right to Remain Anonymous The participant has the right to insist that his or her identity not be revealed or used as a part of any scientific investigation. The research scientist must do everything possible not to reveal the names of participants. This is particularly important when dealing with sensitive issues. The best way to do this is to assign numbers to participants. In particular, we should not use the names of individuals when we report data. In addition, in this age of sophisticated computer hackers, you should also protect the access of individuals to the data files in computers. One way to do this is to have dedicated computers for data storage that are not accessible through the web.

Informed Consent The researcher must inform each participant of the purpose of the research and how the data will be kept confidential. If any risk is involved, physical or psychological, the participant must be informed. Usually researchers use informed consent forms that the participant signs.

The Right to Expect Scientific Responsibility The participant in any study should be certain that the research scientist is not going to endanger his or her mental or physical well-being. To place a subject at risk, physical or psychological, is a violation of the use of human subjects.

Respect for Intellectual Property

A cardinal sin in science is *plagiarism*. Plagiarism is cheating! Plagiarism is an illegal act that involves the direct copying and use of another person's work and words without giving that person proper credit. Plagiarism is stealing someone else's intellectual property. All universities view plagiarism so seriously that it becomes grounds for instant dismissal. Respect the intellectual property of others and acknowledge the other person or persons when you are using their work in informing your research. Place any quoted portion of an author's work, even a sentence, in quotation marks and cite the specific reference, including the page number. You need not place the work of another author that you paraphrase (reword) in quotation marks, but you should still credit the author or authors. We customarily give credit in the following manner: Several authors (Pemberton, 1993; Roberts, 1997; Spink, 1996) have argued that the nature of motivation of athletes is cognitive based.

If you quote from an article, then put it into quotation marks and reference the source with the page number, as follows: An achievement goal is viewed as determining the probability of a person displaying a certain behavior pattern, while "situational factors are seen as potentially altering those probabilities" (Dweck & Leggett, 1988, p. 269).

If you use more than 40 words in a quotation, then place it in a freestanding block as follows:

Relative to the interactionist approach in achievement goal theory, Roberts, Treasure, and Kavussanu (1997) state:

> The results of Swain and Harwood (1996) and Treasure and Roberts (1997) suggest that there is much to be gained from adopting an interactionist approach to the study of motivation in physical activity. The fact that significant main effects emerged for both situational and individual variables in the respective studies appears to confirm the veracity of investigating the effects of goal orientations and perceptions of the motivational climate that the majority of achievement goal research has taken to date (e.g., Duda et al., 1995; Roberts, Treasure & Kavussanu, 1996; Treasure, in press; Walling et al., 1992). Of more interest, perhaps,

was the finding that the interaction of situational and individual variables added to our understanding of the sport experience. Both studies found support for Dweck and Leggett's (1988) contention that situational factors may moderate the effect of goal orientations in determining the probability of adopting a certain goal of action and displaying a particular behavior pattern (p.435).

To avoid plagiarizing, it is better to operate by the adage: Give credit where credit is due.

Conclusion

We have organized the five learning experiences in part I to allow students to search out their questions and to introduce the basic procedures for seeking answers. A basic rule of science is to keep the study simple; this is called parsimony. Often, studies are complex and have complicated analysis procedures, but many classic studies in science are simple and to the point. In the language of science, such experiments are termed elegant. Parsimony should always be the goal.

It is not true that years of experience, multiple academic degrees, and spending much of your life in the library are necessary before you can be a good scholar and conduct good science. In our experience with teaching research methods to sport psychology students for more than 25 years, we have found that undergraduate college students conduct sound research of publishable quality. You can do it, too. You must be curious, industrious, organized, and ethical, and follow the rules of science.

Learning Experience

Purpose

- To understand how to report research to peers.
- To appreciate the organizational structure of a research report.
- To appreciate the logic of a research article.

Procedure

1. Read the article included below and note the following.
2. Pay attention to the information in the introduction. Do the authors present the rationale for doing the research?
3. From the method presented, could you replicate the study?
4. Do the analyses make intuitive sense to you given the rationale the authors present for doing the research?
5. Does the discussion add meaning to the issue under investigation?
6. Have the authors done the research ethically? Would you have had a problem with being a participant in this research?
7. Answer the questions.

Research Article

Orthogonality of Achievement Goals and Its Relationship to Beliefs About Success and Satisfaction in Sport

Glyn C. Roberts

University of Illinois at Urbana-Champaign

Darren C. Treasure

Southern Illinois University at Edwardsville

Maria Kavussanu

Illinois State University

The present study examined the relationship between dispositional achievement goal orientations and satisfaction and beliefs about success in sport. Participants were 333 students who were administered the Perception of Success Questionnaire (POSQ) (Roberts & Balague, 1989, 1991; Roberts, Treasure, & Balague, 1995), Beliefs about Success, and Satisfaction/Interest/Boredom Questionnaires (Duda & Nicholls, 1992). Consistent with theory (Nicholls, 1984, 1989) and previous research, task and ego goal orientations were found to be orthogonal. Following an extreme group split of the task and ego subscales of the POSQ, results of a $2 \times 3 \times 2$ (High/Low Ego; High/Low Task) multivariate analyses of variance revealed a significant interaction effect between task and ego orientation. Specifically, participants high in ego and low in task orientation believed effort to be less a cause of success while high task/ low ego-oriented individuals were the least likely to attribute success to external factors. The findings are discussed in terms of their motivational implications for athletes.

The construct of perceived ability has become one of the central variables attended to by researchers interested in understanding motivation in sport contexts. Generally, the focus has been on how much ability one has relative to others, or how efficacious one feels in certain achievement contexts. But recent research from an achievement goal perspective has clearly established that more than one conception of ability exists and these different conceptions of ability determine one's affective and cognitive responses to achievement outcomes, and influence achievement striving in sport (e.g., Duda, Fox, Biddle, & Armstrong, 1992; Treasure & Roberts, 1994a).

Two conceptions of ability manifest themselves in achievement contexts, namely an undifferentiated concept of ability, where ability and effort are not differentiated by the individual, and a differentiated concept of ability, where ability and effort are differentiated (Nicholls, 1984, 1989). These two conceptions of ability are assumed to be embedded within two achievement goal orientations consistent with the conception of ability adopted. In this paper, the two goal orientations are termed task and ego (Nicholls, 1984, 1989). An individual who is task-oriented uses an undifferentiated conception of ability, and the person's actions are aimed at achieving mastery, learning, and/or perfecting a task. The individual evaluates personal performance to determine whether effort is expended and mastery achieved; thus, the demonstration of ability is self-referenced and success is realized when mastery is demonstrated. In practical terms, this person is task-focused and keeps trying hard even when faced with difficulty and/or defeat. In contrast, an individual who is ego-oriented uses a differentiated conception of ability and the person's actions are aimed at exceeding the performance of others. The individual evaluates personal performance with reference to that of others; thus, the demonstration of ability is other referenced and success is realized when the performance of others is exceeded, especially if little effort is expended (Dweck & Elliott, 1983; Maehr & Braskamp, 1986; Nicholls, 1984, 1989). In practical terms, this person seeks competition with others but is likely to withdraw effort in the face of defeat. Thus, a major difference between an ego- and a task-oriented individual concerns their beliefs about what causes success in achievement contexts.

An important assumption of achievement goal theory is that the goals are orthogonal; that is, task and ego goal orientations are independent, which means one can be high or low in each, or both orientations at the same time. However, most of the research to date has focused on examining the cognitive, affective, and behavioral correlates of being either task- or ego-oriented (e.g., Duda, Chi, Newton, Walling, & Catley, 1995; Lochbaum & Roberts, 1993; Treasure & Roberts, 1994a). An interesting research question, therefore, presents itself and concerns the motivational consequences of different goal orientation profiles. For example, how do individuals who are high in ego orientation and low in task orientation differ from those students who are high in both ego and task orientation?

In the recreational sport domain, Duda (1988) examined the relationship between achievement goal orientation and specific motivated behaviors, such as persistence and behavioral intensity. Based on their orientations to both achievement goals, participants were classified into four groups. A participant was classified as high or low on a certain goal if the participant was at least a half standard deviation above or below the mean, respectively. The results of this study revealed a significant interaction effect between task and ego goal orientation for persistence and behavioral intensity. Specifically, participants who were high on task orientation participated in intramural sport longer, and devoted more time to practice their intramural sport irrespective of their level of ego orientation. It is interesting to note that it was the high ego/low task-oriented group that reported devoting the least amount of time to practice. Interpreting these results, Duda (1988) argues a high-task orientation provides the participant with mastery standards to fall back on if he/she is not the best at a specific task or the desired extrinsic reinforcements are no longer present. Duda concludes that an individual who is high in both task and ego goal orientation has two sources of success and several reasons to continue his or her participation in an activity.

In the context of physical education, Walling and Duda (1995) found students high in ego orientation were more likely than low ego-oriented students to express the belief that success is achieved when they possess high ability. In addition, high task-oriented students were significantly more likely to believe that success is achieved through intrinsic interest in the activity and high effort than low task-oriented students. Finally, high task/low ego students were the least likely to believe that success stems from learning to skillfully deceive the teacher.

The purpose of the present study, therefore, was to examine Nicholls' (1984, 1989) proposal that task and ego goal orientations are orthogonal and interact to effect an individual's cognitive and affective responses. Specifically, the present study focused on the participants' beliefs about the causes of success and satisfaction in sport, variables that are considered to exert considerable influence on the direction of achievement behavior, and the quality of involvement (Ames, 1992; Nicholls, 1989). It was expected we would replicate the main effects observed by previous research (e.g., Duda et al., 1995; Roberts & Ommundsen, 1996) and find a high-task orientation to be related to the belief that the cause of success is effort, and that high task-oriented individuals experience more satisfaction when trying hard. In contrast, it was hypothesized that high ego-oriented individuals would endorse the belief that the cause of success is ability and that these individuals derive satisfaction from outperforming others. Extending previous research on the correlates of task and ego goal orientations, we also expected to find interaction effects, and hypothesized that individuals who were high in a task orientation would be satisfied with the sport experience, and endorse both effort and ability as causes of success irrespective of their level of ego orientation (Duda, 1988). However, individuals who were low in both task and ego orientations were expected to be more bored with the sport experience (Walling & Duda, 1995).

Method

Participants and Procedure

The participants for this study were 106 female and 227 male undergraduate students (mean age = 20.97 years; range 18-44 years), attending a large university in the Midwest of the United States. Participants who had competitive sport experience were recruited from physical activity classes and reported an average 11.27 years of participation in competitive sport (range 1 to 34 years). Participants were administered three questionnaires: one assessing goal orientation; a second assessing beliefs about success in sport; and a third assessing satisfaction, interest, and boredom in sport. Normal informed-consent procedures were followed. After detailed written instructions were provided to the instructors, questionnaires were administered to participants by the class instructors. Participants were assured their responses would be kept anonymous and were encouraged to answer the questions as honestly as possible with reference to their competitive sport experience.

Questionnaires

Goal Orientations

The Perception of Success Questionnaire (POSQ) (Roberts & Balague, 1989, 1991; Roberts, Treasure, & Balague, in press) was used to assess dispositional goal orientation. The POSQ has been developed as a sport-specific questionnaire to measure goal orientations. It is a 12-item scale consisting of two subscales measuring task and ego goals and has demonstrated acceptable validity and reliability in previous research (see Roberts & Balague, 1989, 1991; Roberts, Treasure, & Balague, in press; Roberts & Treasure, 1995; Treasure & Roberts, 1994b). Participants responded to a 5-point Likert scale ranging from strongly disagree (1) to strongly agree (5). The stem for each item was "I feel most successful in sport when . . . ." Examples of items constituting the ego subscale are as follows: "I show other people I am the best," "I am clearly superior." Examples of items constituting the task subscale are as follows: "I show clear personal improvement," "I reach personal goals." Participants' scores are calculated by adding their responses (1 through 5) for each item on the respective scales, and dividing by the number of items in each subscale. Thus, a separate score is calculated for each subscale. In the present study, the two subscales were found to be internally reliable with alpha coefficients of .80 and .86 for the task and ego subscales, respectively (Cronbach, 1951). The intercorrelation of $r = .08$ between the two subscales confirmed the proposed orthogonality of the two goal orientations (Nicholls, 1984, 1989).

Beliefs About Success

A 17-item questionnaire (Duda & Nicholls, 1992) was used to assess participants' beliefs about causes of success in sport, and has demonstrated adequate reliability and validity. Specifically, participants were asked what they think helps people do well and succeed in sport. Responses were indicated in a 5-point Likert scale ranging from strongly disagree (1) to strongly agree (5). The questionnaire consisted of three subscales assessing participants' beliefs that success stems from (a) motivation/effort (e.g., "They work really hard," "They like to learn new skills"); (b) ability (e.g., "They are better at sport than others," "They were born naturally good at sport"); and (c) deception/external factors (e.g., "They are lucky," "They know how to impress the coach"). Participants' scores for each subscale were calculated by adding their responses (1 through 5) in each item, and dividing by the number of items. The subscales demonstrated internal reliabilities of .80, .61, and .73 for the motivation/effort, ability, and deception/external factors subscales, respectively. Because the ability subscale demonstrated inadequate internal consistency, it was eliminated from further analyses.

Satisfaction/Interest/Boredom

The degree of satisfaction with and interest in sport were assessed using an 8-item inventory developed by Nicholls and his colleagues (Duda & Nicholls, 1992; Nicholls, Patashnick, & Nolen, 1985; Nicholls, Cheung, Lauer, & Patashnick, 1989). This inventory has demonstrated adequate validity and reliability, and incorporates a 5-item enjoyment/interest subscale and a 3-item boredom subscale. Items such as "I usually enjoy playing sport" constitute the enjoyment/interest subscale, whereas items such as "When playing sport I am usually bored" constitute the boredom subscale. Previous research has indicated that although these subscales are related, they are not bi-polar opposites of the same construct (Duda et al., 1992). On this occasion they were found to be internally reliable (alphas were .84 and .71 for the satisfaction/interest and the boredom subscales, respectively) and moderately correlated ($r = +.54$).

Results

As previous research has demonstrated that men and women differ in their strength of task and ego goal orientations (e.g., Duda, 1989; Duda et al., 1995), we conducted a one-way analysis of variance (ANOVA) procedure to assess gender differences in task and ego goal orientations. Consistent with Duda, men ($M = 3.76$, $SD = .76$) were higher in ego orientation than women ($M = 3.55$, $SD = .82$), $F(1,332) = 5.61$, $p < .05$. In contrast, women ($M = 4.68$, $SD = .45$) were higher in task orientation than men ($M = 4.53$, $SD = .45$), $F(1,332) = 9.14$, $p < .01$. Although the gender differences were statistically significant, the slight mean differences (.21 for ego orientation and .15 for task orientation) make one wonder if the differences are meaningful or simply reflect sample size. To assess the meaningfulness of the gender differences, we calculated effect sizes (ES) for task and ego goal orientation. Based on the standards advocated by Cohen (1977), an effect size of 0.2 was considered a small ES, 0.4 to 0.6 a moderate ES, and 0.7 and above a large ES. As the ESs for ego and task goal orientations in this instance were +.27 and .33, respectively, it was considered appropriate to collapse men and women into one group for the purpose of this study.

Canonical Correlations

It was hypothesized that participants' achievement goal orientations would be linked to their beliefs about the causes of success and satisfaction/interest/boredom in sport in a conceptually coherent fashion. In order to assess the nature of these multivariate relationships, a canonical analysis was conducted. Two significant canonical functions emerged (Wilks' lambda = .66; $r_{c1} = .53$ for Function 1 and $r_{c2} = .25$ for Function 2).[1] The strength of the relationship between the participants' goal orientations and their beliefs about the causes of success and satisfaction/interest/boredom in sport can be observed through the redundancy statistic. A redundancy value of 10% or greater is considered significant and meaningful (Pedhazur, 1982; Tabachnick & Fidell, 1989). The total redundancy statistic revealed that 58.8% of the variance in the criterion variables could be explained by the set of predictor variables. As the amount of variance explained by Function 1 (33.2%) and Function 2 (25.6%) suggests, two solutions could explain the nature of the relationships among the variables; thus, both functions were analyzed.

The canonical loadings represent the contribution of each of the variables in a set to the multivariate relationships. Values greater than .30 were considered to be significant contributors to the multivariate relationships (Pedhazur, 1982; Tabachnick & Fidell, 1989). For the criterion set, there was a high positive loading for task orientation and a low negative loading for ego orientation. In order of magnitude, loadings for the predictor variables for Function 1 indicated that believing effort causes success, experiencing satisfaction/interest and boredom, and believing external factors cause success contributed most significantly to the multivariate relationship. These loadings reflect a strong, conceptually coherent relationship between the participants' task goal orientation and their cognitive and affective responses. Specifically, task-oriented participants were those who believed effort, rather than external factors, caused success, and experienced satisfaction/interest and not boredom during their sport experience.

A high positive loading for ego orientation and a low moderate loading for task orientation emerged for the criterion variables for Function 2. In order of magnitude, loadings for the predictor variables indicated that experiencing satisfaction/interest and believing external factors cause success in sport contributed most significantly to the multivariate relationship. Consistent with Function 1, these loadings indicate there was a strong relationship between the participants' goal orientation and their cognitive and affective responses.

Group Comparisons

Achievement goal theory postulates that task and ego goal orientations are orthogonal, which means an individual may be high and/or low in each goal orientation at any given time. As stated above, and assessed by the correlational and canonical procedures, to date most research has examined the cognitive, affective, and behavioral consequences of adopting either a task or an ego goal orientation. In the present study, we wished to assess the possible interaction of the two goal orientations. To this end, we constructed an extreme group split, +/− half a standard deviation of the median score (task MD 4.66, SD .43; ego MD 3.75, SD .786), on the participants' responses to the task and ego subscales of the POSQ. We then conducted a $2 \times 3 \times 2$ (high/low ego 3 high/low task) Multivariate Analysis of Variance (MANOVA) with the participants' beliefs about the causes of success and satisfaction/interest/boredom in sport as the dependent variables. As expected, a significant multivariate main effect emerged for task orientation (Wilks' lambda = .67; $F(4,99) = 12.03$, $p < .001$). Follow-up univariate analyses revealed significant differences between those participants high or low in task orientation on 3 of the 4 dependent variables. Specifically, high task-oriented participants ($M = 4.62$, $SD = .35$), regardless of level of ego orientation, believed effort to be a cause of success significantly more so than low task-oriented participants ($M = 4.03$, $SD = .53$), $F(1,195) = 84.68$, $p < .001$ (ES = 1.3). High task-oriented participants also reported experiencing significantly more satisfaction/interest ($M = 4.70$, $SD = .43$), than low task-oriented participants ($M = 4.31$, $SD = .65$), $F(1,195) = 26.43$, $p < .001$ (ES = .71). Consistent with this, high task-oriented participants ($M = 1.72$, $SD = .60$) reported feeling less boredom than low task-oriented participants ($M = 2.00$, $SD = .78$), $F(1,195) = 8.61$, $p < .005$ (ES = +.41). The multivariate main effect for ego orientation was not significant (Wilks' lambda = .91; $F(4,99) = 2.36$, $p = .58$).

However, this analysis was superseded by a significant multivariate interaction effect (Wilks' lambda = .91; $F(4,99) = 2.51$, $p < .05$. Follow-up univariate analyses revealed that believing success to be caused by effort, $F(1,102) = 3.69$, $p < .05$, and external factors, $F(1,102) = 5.12$, $p < .01$, were responsible for the multivariate interaction. Examination of the simple main effects for effort reveals the group where participants who were high in ego and low in task orientation believed effort to be less a cause of success than the other groups. Evidently, being high in task as well as high in ego orientation was sufficient to modify the predilection of high-ego participants to discount effort as a cause of success. Congruent with the results for effort, examination of the simple main effects for external factors as a cause of success reveals the participants who were high in task and low in ego orientation were least likely to attribute success to external factors. Being low in task and/or high in ego orientation was sufficient to make external factors more likely to be attributed for success.

Discussion

First, the psychometric analyses of the present study confirmed the reliability of POSQ to determine the achievement goal orientations of individuals when reflecting on their perception of success in competitive sport experiences, and provided additional support for the veracity of POSQ to measure achievement goals in sport contexts (Roberts & Balague, 1989, 1991; Roberts & Treasure, 1995; Roberts, Treasure, Balague, in press; Treasure & Roberts, 1994b). Further, consistent with previous research (Ames & Archer, 1988; Roberts & Treasure, 1995; Treasure & Roberts, 1994a), the present study found the ego and task goal orientations were orthogonal ($r = .08$).

The main effect findings of the present study are consistent with previous research that has shown achievement goal orientations provide a meaningful way of differentiating the beliefs and affect of individuals within the competitive sport experience (e.g., Duda & Nicholls, 1992; Lochbaum & Roberts, 1993; Roberts & Treasure, 1995; Treasure & Roberts, 1994a; Walling & Duda, 1995). Specifically, in the present study, high task-oriented individuals believed effort to be a cause of success and experienced more satisfaction than low task-oriented individuals. In contrast, high ego-oriented individuals believed external factors, such as impressing the coach, to be associated with success in sport and were satisfied with the sport experience.

However, it was the significant interaction effect that supported the primary thesis of the present study. When we partialed out the sources of the interaction by investigating the simple main effects, we found that reliable differences occurred for effort as a cause of success, and for external factors as a cause of success. For the endorsement of effort as a cause of success, an important variable in achievement goal theory, we found that although being high in ego orientation is usually associated with discounting effort as a cause of success (e.g., Duda, 1989; Treasure & Roberts, 1994a), when high-ego individuals also were high in task orientation, this was sufficient to mediate the belief high ego-oriented individuals typically hold. In the present study, we found that high ego/high task-oriented individuals exhibited the same adaptive beliefs as the high task/low ego-oriented individuals.

In past research, it has been usual for investigators to deplore being high in ego orientation and suggest that we do our utmost to depress ego orientation and enhance task orientation instead (e.g., Duda, 1992, 1993; Roberts, 1992, 1993). However, the present research suggests we enhance task orientation *as well* for high ego-oriented individuals. Rather than replacing ego with task orientation, it seems we can achieve similar results by enhancing task orientation. This is an interesting finding and is intuitively appealing. It has always been a difficult task to convince coaches to depress ego orientation as many coaches implicitly, and explicitly, believe it is necessary to be ego-oriented to achieve excellence and competitive success. If we can argue, as the data herein support, that we have no need to depress ego orientation, that we can enhance task orientation to moderate the potentially debilitating effects of high-ego orientation, then this is a more plausible avenue to take. As Duda (1988) suggests, it gives the high task/high ego-oriented athlete more criteria with which to assess success.

The second reliable simple main effect was that individuals who were high in task and low in ego orientation were the least likely to endorse external factors as a cause of success. This finding again supports the notion that we need to know the level of both task and ego orientation to fully understand the motivational implications of holding beliefs about the causes of success. Being high in ego and/or low in task was sufficient to make external factors more salient. In this case, being high in task and low in ego was the crucial contribution. We failed to replicate the findings of Walling and Duda (1995) who found those participants who were low in both task and ego orientation scored lower than others on the scales used. Walling and Duda were interested in the purposes of and beliefs about success in physical education, while we investigated satisfaction and beliefs about success in sport, which may account for the differences. But, in the present study, we did not find these individuals to be most at-risk from a motivational point of view. Rather, that distinction belonged to the high ego- and low task-oriented athletes. These were the ones who were most likely to exhibit the beliefs and cognitions that would place them at-risk motivationally.

Conclusion

An important assumption of achievement goal theory is that the goals are conceptually orthogonal. We confirmed that with these findings. However, of the variables we investigated, only two contributed to the multivariate interaction effect. We failed to find the hypothesized satisfaction effects, but we did confirm the beliefs about success hypotheses underscoring the importance of holding a high-task orientation. Other research has endorsed high-task orientation as a desirable motivational attribute (e.g., Walling & Duda, 1995). However, the implication has always been that the high-task orientation replace a high-ego orientation. This research suggests a high-task orientation complements a high-ego orientation. This is further underscored by the fact that the athletes most at-risk motivationally in the present study were the high ego/ low task-oriented. Therefore, finding a means to enhance task-oriented criteria is important as it tempers the high-ego orientation. Clearly, coaches would be well advised to advocate tasks involving criteria of success for athletes, whether the athletes are high or low in ego orientation.

References

Ames, C. (1992). Achievement goals in the classroom: Students' learning strategies and motivation processes. *Journal of Educational Psychology*, 79, 409-414.

Ames, C., & Archer, J. (1988). Achievement goals in the classroom: Students' learning strategies and motivation processes. *Journal of Educational Psychology*, 79, 409-414.

Cohen, J. (1977). *Statistical power analysis for the behavioral sciences.* New York: Academic Press.

Cronbach, L.J. (1951). Coefficient alpha and the internal structure of tests. *Psychometrika*, 16, 297-334.

Duda, J.L. (1988). The relationship between goal perspectives, persistence, and behavioral intensity among male and female recreational sport participants. *Leisure Sciences*, 10, 95-106.

Duda, J.L. (1989). The relationship between task and ego orientation and the perceived purpose of sport among male and female high school athletes. *Journal of Sport & Exercise Psychology*, 11, 318-335.

Duda, J.L. (1993). Goals: A social cognitive approach to the study of achievement motivation in sport. In R.N. Singer, M. Murphey, & L.K. Tennant (Eds.), *Handbook of research on sport psychology* (pp. 421-436). St. Louis, MO: McMillan.

Duda, J.L., & Nicholls, J.G. (1992). Dimensions of achievement motivation in schoolwork and sport. *Journal of Educational Psychology*, 84, 290-299.

Duda, J.L., Fox, K.R., Biddle, S.J.H., & Armstrong, N. (1992). Children's achievement goals and beliefs about success in sport. *British Journal of Educational Psychology*, 84, 290-299.

Duda, J.L., Chi, L., Newton, M.L., Walling, M.D., & Catley, D. (1995). Task and ego orientation and intrinsic motivation in sport. *International Journal of Sport Psychology*, 26, 40-63.

Dweck, C.S., & Elliott, E.S. (1983). Achievement motivation. In E.M. Hetherington (Ed.), *Handbook of child psychology: Vol. 4. Socialization, personality, and social development* (pp. 643-691). New York: Wiley.

Lochbaum, M.R., & Roberts, G.C. (1993). Goal orientations and perceptions of the sport experience. *Journal of Sport & Exercise Psychology*, 15, 160-171.

Maehr, M., & Braskamp, L.A. (1986). *The motivational factor: A theory of personal investment.* Lexington, MA: Lexington Books.

Nicholls, J.G. (1984). Achievement motivation: Conceptions of ability, subjective experience, task choice, and performance. *Psychological Review*, 91(3), 328-346.

Nicholls, J.G. (1989). *The competitive ethos and democratic education.* Cambridge, MA: Harvard University Press.

Nicholls, J.G., Cheung, P.C., Lauer, J., & Patashnick, M. (1989). Individual differences in academic motivation: Perceived ability, goals, beliefs, and values. *Learning and Individual Differences*, 1, 63-84.

Nicholls, J.G., Patashnick, M., & Nolen, S.B. (1985). Adolescents' theories of education. *Journal of Educational Psychology*, 77, 683-692.

Pedhazur, E.J. (1982). *Multiple regression in behavioral research.* New York: Holt, Rinehart & Winston.

Roberts, G.C. (1992). Motivation in sport and exercise: Conceptual constraints and convergence. In G.C. Roberts (Ed.), *Motivation in sport and exercise* (pp. 3-30). Champaign, IL: Human Kinetics.

Roberts, G.C. (1993). Motivation in sport: Understanding and enhancing the motivation and achievement of children. In R.N. Singer, M. Murphey, & L.K. Tennant (Eds.), *Handbook of research on sport psychology* (pp. 405-420). St. Louis, MO: McMillan.

Roberts, G.C., & Balague, G. (1989, August). *The development of a social cognitive scale of motivation.* Paper presented at the 7th World Congress of Sport Psychology, Singapore.

Roberts, G.C., & Balague, G. (1991, September). *The development and validation of the perception of success questionnaire.* Paper presented in the 10th FEPSAC European Congress of Sport Psychology, Cologne, Germany.

Roberts, G.C., & Ommundsen, Y. (1996). Effect of goal orientations on achievement beliefs, cognitions, and strategies in team sport. *Scandinavian Journal of Medicine and Science in Sports,* 6, 46-56.

Roberts, G.C., Treasure, D.C., & Balague, G. (in press). Achievement goals in sport: The development and validation of the Perception of Success Questionnaire. *Journal of Sport Sciences.*

Roberts, G.C., & Treasure, D.C. (1995). Achievement goals, motivational climate, and achievement strategies and behaviors in sport. *International Journal of Sport Psychology.* 10, 398-408.

Tabachnick, B.G., & Fidell, L.S. (1989). *Using multivariate statistics.* New York: Harper & Row.

Treasure, D.C., & Roberts, G.C. (1994a). Cognitive and affective concomitants of task and ego goal orientations during the middle school years. *Journal of Sport & Exercise Psychology,* 16, 15-28.

Treasure, D.C., & Roberts, G.C. (1994b). Perception of Success Questionnaire: Preliminary validation in an adolescent population. *Perceptual and Motor Skills,* 79, 607-610.

Walling, M., & Duda, J.L. (1995). Goals and their associations with beliefs about success in and perceptions of the purposes of physical education. *Journal of Teaching Physical Education,* 14, 140-156.

Manuscript submitted: September 1995

Revision received: July 1996

Questions

Write answers to the following questions. Be prepared to discuss the answers at the next learning experience meeting.

1. What was the purpose of the study? Did the authors clearly state the rationale for the study?
2. Was the literature review pertinent to the question?
3. How recent were the cited works in the review? Were they from scholarly journals or from the popular media?
4. From the methodology presented, could you replicate this study?
5. Who were the participants for this study?
6. Did the authors conduct the study ethically and did they protect the rights of the participants?
7. How do you know?
8. Did the authors conduct the study so the data were reliable and valid?
9. How do you know?
10. Were the questionnaires valid for this study?
11. Did the authors make any attempt to demonstrate validity?
12. What were the dependent variables, and were they pertinent to the question?
13. What were the independent variables, and did they capture the essential purpose of the study?
14. From your limited experience at this point, did the data analysis procedures make sense and were they explained adequately?
15. What findings could you list from the study?
16. Did the findings support the hypotheses the researchers stated?
17. Did the authors present the data in a way that helped you understand the findings?
18. Did the discussion help you understand the significance of the research?
19. Did the authors place the findings into perspective by referring to previous research?
20. If you had to describe the findings of the research study in one sentence, what would you write?

Suggested Reading

For more information, consult the following references:

American Psychological Association. (1994). *Publication manual of the American Psychological Association* (4th ed.). Washington, DC: Author.

Kerlinger, F. (1973). *Foundations of behavioral research.* New York: Holt, Rinehart & Winston.

Thomas, J. & Nelson, J. (1996). *Research methods in physical activity.* (3rd ed.) Champaign, IL: Human Kinetics.

PART 2

UNDERSTANDING SPORT PSYCHOLOGICAL PHENOMENA

EXPERIENCE 6

SOCIAL FACILITATION

What is the one thing that most sport performances have in common? Spectators, of course! Most sport events, whether Little League baseball or professional basketball, take place in front of crowds. The people present may be a small group of family and friends or a huge arena full of worshipping fans. We have all heard of the so-called home court advantage, but have you ever wondered about the psychological processes that allow spectators to influence an athlete's performance? The impact may be negative. For example, John plays well during practice when few people are there to watch, but during games with spectators present his performance drops dramatically. On the other hand, spectators seem to enhance the performance of others. Sue performs much better in front of a crowd than during practice when spectators are absent. How is it that crowds facilitate the performance of one athlete but inhibit the performance of another? Sport psychologists have studied this process under the heading of *social facilitation*.

Objectives

In this learning experience you will learn

- about the phenomenon of social facilitation,
- about a model explaining why social facilitation may hinder or enhance performance,
- about research findings in the area of sport and motor learning, and
- some concerns about social facilitation.

Then you will have the opportunity to conduct a learning experience in the form of an experiment to determine the effect of the presence of others on motor performance.

Basic Considerations

Social facilitation research is concerned with the effect of the presence of others on an individual's performance. Present others may be defined in two ways: (a) the audience situation, in which spectators are observing an individual, or (b) the coaction situation, in which two or more individuals are performing the same task at the same time. Sport contains many situations involving coaction (e.g., a swimming or running race), audiences (e.g., spectators at a boxing match), and elements of both (spectators watching a marathon), which make the presence of others an important phenomenon to investigate and understand in sport.

Interest in the effects on performance induced by the presence of others dates back to 1898, when it was the subject of a classic study conducted by Triplett. The investigator noted that bicycle riders appeared to cycle faster in groups than they did alone. To investigate this phenomenon, Triplett conducted an experiment in which subjects wound fishing reels for speed, either alone or paired with another person. He found that paired subjects performed better than those winding reels alone.

Following Triplett's seminal work, other early research produced equivocal results. Although several studies supported Triplett's finding that performance on various tasks could be enhanced by the presence of either coactors or passive spectators (e.g., Dashiell, 1930; Leuba, 1933), others found that present others impaired performance (e.g., Pessin, 1933). Whenever we get contradictory findings like this, it becomes a challenge for psychologists to determine why.

This challenge was finally met by Zajonc in 1965 when he used drive theory to provide an explanation. As with many good psychological theories, the explanation was simple and easily understood. Zajonc argued that the presence of others is, in itself, arousing. Arousal enhances the emission of dominant responses relative to subordinate ones (Spence, 1956). On simple or well-learned tasks, correct responses are assumed to be dominant, but on complex or unlearned tasks, incorrect responses are assumed to be dominant. A person learning a new and difficult task does not know how to consistently do it correctly; hence, arousal generated by others present in the learning situation makes performance worse because it facilitates the incorrect response. When the person becomes skilled at the task, however, the presence of others arouses him or her and the pressure makes the performance better, because arousal facilitates the correct response. Thus, arousal enhances simple or well-learned tasks but impairs complex or unlearned tasks. Zajonc and Sales (1966) provided evidence of this learning and performance dichotomy.

Using a motor skill, Martens (1969) provided further evidence to support Zajonc. Martens had a group of subjects perform an unlearned motor task either in front of an audience or alone. The group who performed in front of the audience had impaired performance, which supports predictions. Martens had the same group of subjects continue to learn the task until they could perform it well. These subjects then performed the task either in front of an audience or alone and, as predicted, the audience group performed better. In addition, using the Palmar Sweat Index, Martens found that subjects who performed before an audience demonstrated a higher level of physiological arousal than did those who performed alone. It seems that the social facilitation effects are a function of the arousal generated by the presence of others.

Subsequent research, however, suggests that the presence of other persons is not, by itself, sufficient to produce the social facilitation effect. Cottrell (1968) disagreed with Zajonc and argued that arousal was generated by present others because they could *evaluate* the performance of the subjects. Cottrell stated that everyone is subjected to evaluative experiences that lead to the anticipation of positive or negative outcomes in the presence of others. Further, this expectation of evaluation may be the necessary condition for the social facilitation effect. Many studies support this proposition (e.g., Haas & Roberts, 1975; Martens & Landers, 1972). In these studies, the social facilitation effect depends on subjects' perceptions that their performance was being evaluated by the present others.

Another point of contention in the area of social facilitation concerns the equivalence of the coaction and audience effects. In Zajonc's (1965) original formulation, the effect of the presence of coactors and an audience was assumed to be equivalent. This assumption has been challenged by Landers and McCullagh (1976). These authors suggest that, in the coaction situation, performers have an opportunity to pick up additional information from coactors because they can see how their fellow learners are completing the task. These are directive cues concerning the most useful performance strategy and are not available to learners with the audience situation. This reasoning has intuitive appeal (e.g., imagine practicing a new skill such as a draw on a golf shot at the same time as someone else, versus practicing alone in front of an audience). It may explain why studies comparing the two situations have found different results (Bird, 1973). From investigating this phenomenon specifically, Seta (1982) found that participants' performance improved when they were paired with coactors performing at slightly superior levels, but performance was not influenced by the presence of coactors performing at inferior, identical, or very superior levels.

These findings suggest that audience and coaction situations may differ. We need to direct more research toward explaining the behavioral effects of the presence of coactors versus spectators. The learning experience provides an opportunity to investigate this question.

Learning Experience

Purpose

To compare the times of individuals performing a simple muscular endurance task in a coaction situation with individuals performing in front of an audience.

Measuring Tools

A strong wall, a stopwatch, and the Social Facilitation Data Sheet on page 70.

The Task

The person performs a muscular endurance task called the skier's squat. Perform this task as follows:

1. The participant stands about 18 in. from a wall (facing away from the wall) with feet shoulder-width.

2. The participant leans back against the wall and slides downward until reaching a sitting position (with knees bent at 90°).

3. The participant folds his or her arms across the chest.

4. The participant's objective is to maintain the position (with knees at 90°) for as long as possible.

5. An experimenter, using a stopwatch, times and records the trial for each participant to the nearest 10th of a second. The time for each trial starts when the participant's knees are bent 90° and ends when the participant's knees deviate from 90°.

Procedure

1. Randomly divide the class into three equal groups. Ensure balanced sex distribution.

2. Designate Group 1 as the experimenter's group. They will be the spectators for Group 2.

3. Designate Group 2 as the audience group. Members of this group perform the skier's squat one at a time in front of the spectators (Group 1). One experimenter (from Group 1) times each participant and records the time the participant maintains the skier's squat position. The spectators remain passive throughout the trial.

4. Designate Group 3 as the coacting group. Participants in this group perform the skier's squat in a coacting group of four (it can be less than four but more than one). Each group of four performs together in the presence of one experimenter (from Group 1), who times each participant in the group and records the time that he or she maintained the position. For four coactors, the experimenter will record four separate times.

5. Transfer all the times recorded for the participants in the audience and coacting groups to the data sheet on page 70.

Analysis of Results

To test whether differences exist between the two means (Groups 2 and 3), a t-test for independent groups is necessary. We run a t-test on data to clearly establish whether the difference between the means of the two groups is attributable to chance. (Review page 38 for the t-test.) Complete the formula to obtain t. Use the Social Facilitation Data Sheet to determine whether a real difference exists between the groups.

Discussion Questions

1. What does the obtained *t*-statistic mean in this study?

2. Does the data of this experience pertain to learning or to a performance situation?

3. Did your results support the speculation of Landers and McCullagh (1976)? Explain.

4. When an individual is learning a task, will putting him or her in a competitive situation facilitate learning or inhibit learning? Why?

5. Why would an individual in an athletic setting do well in practice but perform badly in an athletic contest? What could you do about it?

References

Bird, A.M. (1973). Effects of social facilitation upon females' performance of own psychomotor tasks. *Research Quarterly, 44,* 322-330.

Cottrell, N. (1968). Performance in the presence of other human beings: Mere presence, audience and affiliation effects. In E. Simmell, R.A. Hoppe, & G. Milton (Eds.), *Social facilitation and imitative behavior* (pp. 91-110). Boston: Allyn & Bacon.

Dashiell, J.F. (1930). An experimental analysis of some group effects. *Journal of Abnormal and Social Psychology, 25,* 190-199.

Haas, J., & Roberts, G.C. (1975). Effect of evaluative others upon learning and performance of a complex motor task. *Journal of Motor Behavior, 7,* 81-90.

Landers, D.L., & McCullagh, P.D. (1976). Social facilitation of motor performance. In J.F. Keogh (Ed.), *Exercise and sport sciences review* (Vol. 4, pp.125-162). New York: Academic Press.

Leuba, C.J. (1933). An experimental study of rivalry in young children. *Journal of Comparative Psychology, 16,* 367-378.

Martens, R. (1969). Palmar sweating and the presence of an audience. *Journal of Experimental Social Psychology, 5,* 371-374.

Martens, R., & Landers, D.M. (1972). Evaluation potential as a determinant of coaction effects. *Journal of Personality and Social Psychology, 8,* 347-359.

Pessin, J. (1933). The comparative effects of social and mechanical stimulation on memorying. *American Journal of Psychology, 45,* 263-270.

Seta, J.J. (1982). The impact of comparison processes on coactors task performance. *Journal of Personality and Social Psychology, 42,* 281-291.

Spence, K.W. (1956). *Behavior theory and conditioning.* New Haven, CT: Yale University Press.

Triplett, N. (1898). The dynamogenic factors in pace making and competition. *American Journal of Psychology, 9,* 507-533.

Zajonc, R.B. (1965). Social facilitation. *Science, 149,* 259-274.

Zajonc, R.B., & Sales, S. (1966). Social facilitation of dominant and subordinate responses. *Journal of Experimental Social Psychology, 2,* 160-168.

Social Facilitation Data Sheet

Alone (X)		Coacting (Y)	
Name	Time	Name	Time

Complete the following table from the data above.

Alone time (X_1)	X^2	Coacting time (Y_2)	Y^2

$\overline{X}_1 =$ $(\Sigma X)^2 =$ $\Sigma X^2 =$ $\overline{Y}_2 =$ $(\Sigma Y)^2 =$ $\Sigma Y^2 =$

Compute the *t*-statistic using the following formula:

$$t = \frac{\overline{X}_1 - \overline{Y}_2}{\sqrt{\dfrac{S_1^2}{n_1} + \dfrac{S_2^2}{n_2}}}$$

See table for *t*-statistic on page 44.

EXPERIENCE 7

SOCIAL REINFORCEMENT

Have you ever reacted to a fellow athlete's winning goal or basket by saying, "Good job," or patting him or her on the back? What about your reaction to a fellow athlete's poor pass or unnecessary penalty? Possibly you frowned or made a comment such as, "That was pitiful!" If you are like most people, you probably find it hard not to react to other people's behavior in these or similar ways. When you do, you are using a social reinforcer.

Objectives

In this learning experience you will learn

- the definition of social reinforcement and the distinction between negative and positive reinforcement,
- the relationship between social reinforcement and performance, and
- the relationship between social reinforcement and psychological factors.

Then you will have the opportunity to categorize the reinforcements the coach gives at a practice session.

Basic Considerations

What are social reinforcers? They are forms of social reward and punishment, given either verbally or nonverbally to an individual by at least one person who is present. A nod, a pat on the back, or a compliment are examples of social reward; a scowl, a sarcastic comment, or a direct criticism are examples of social punishment.

It should come as no surprise that teachers, coaches, and parents continually use social reinforcers (both reward and punishment) to change behavior. Social reinforcement as a reward is used typically to maintain or increase a response an individual makes. Specifically, if a hockey player refrains from retaliating after being elbowed by an opponent and the coach says, "nice control" (reward), the player is likely to repeat that behavior to receive more positive comments. Social reinforcement as a punishment, on the other hand, is used to extinguish or change an individual's behavior. Following with the hockey example, if a player is berated (punishment) by the coach for retaliating after receiving an elbow from an opponent, the player is likely not to repeat the retaliatory behavior to avoid more negative comments.

Clearly, the coach is a powerful agent for delivering social reinforcement to players of all ages, but little research has investigated the mechanics of the reinforcement process in such environments.

By far the most systematic research on social reinforcement in field settings has been conducted by Smith and Smoll (cf. Smith, Smoll, Hunt, Curtis, & Coppel, 1979) at the University of Washington. Their large-scale project has investigated the behavior of coaches in Little League baseball. It has not focused on social reinforcement per se, but the results of the research have implications for coaches using social reinforcement. Smith et al. found that behaviors classifiable as social reinforcement constitute 43% of all coaching behaviors. Although social reinforcement is obviously an important element of coaching behavior, we need more research on its effect on children in organized sport programs. However, some things we do know are listed here.

To be effective in modifying behavior, social reinforcement must be applied to the specific behaviors to be changed or modified. In other words, contingent social reinforcement is required. In terms of amount, constant praise or constant criticism will not be effective, because the individual cannot distinguish between appropriate and inappropriate behaviors. If constant reinforcement is not appropriate, this begs the question of how much reinforcement should be given. Interestingly, the results of research have revealed that it is not the frequency of reinforcement that is the key, but rather its quality (e.g., appropriateness, contingency, specificity) that will have greatest impact on the individual's performance (Horn, 1992).

From a coaching perspective, it is interesting that research has revealed that the reinforcement coaches give tends to change with athletes who differ in ability levels (Solomon, Striegel, Eliot, Heon, Maas, & Wayda, 1996) or level of sport (Spink, 1988). This suggests that situational factors are a critical element in understanding the effects of reinforcement on individual behavior.

The sequencing of the feedback also appears to influence player performance. Kirschenbaum and Smith (1983) found that continuous feedback (whether positive or negative) was associated with performance decrements, compared with mixed feedback and control conditions. Individuals who received mixed feedback or no feedback performed significantly better on a modified free-throw shooting task than did those who received a continuous regimen of either positive or negative feedback. Thus, continuous positive feedback may produce the same adverse effects as continuous negative feedback. Although we should not take this result to mean that a coach should abandon regularly using positive feedback, it might suggest that feedback is most effective when it is mixed. In terms of the proportion of a positive to negative mix, it has been suggested that 80% to 90% of reinforcement should be positive (Weinberg & Gould, 1995).

In terms of its effects on psychological development, Vallerand (1983) found that low, moderate, and high levels of positive feedback increased an athlete's feelings of competence. Positive feedback, therefore, plays an important indirect role in learning or performing a skill. It conveys to the individual that he or she is competent (cf. Black & Weiss, 1992). The individual is then likely to show higher levels of intrinsic motivation (see experience12, Intrinsic Motivation), and this influences the performance levels attained. In related research, it was found that positive feedback facilitated the confidence levels of females performing physical activity tasks (Petruzzello & Corbin, 1988).

Unfortunately, other research provides little information that we can use effectively in teaching and coaching. However, social reinforcement should not be set aside because we do not fully understand the mechanics. Indeed, because social reinforcement is such a commonly accepted aspect of the teaching-learning environment, it is important to know how social reinforcers might establish a better learning climate. The learning experience offers an opportunity to observe the reinforcements a coach provides to his or her team during a typical practice setting and to see whether the coach has established a good learning environment.

Learning Experience

Purpose

To observe a children's organized sport experience, record the type and number of social reinforcements the coach provides, and categorize those reinforcements.

Measuring Tool

Social Reinforcement Data Sheet, page 77.

Procedure

The scale you will use is loosely based on the Smith and Smoll Coaching Behavior Assessment System (CBAS). Although the original scale has 12 categories, you will use only the following 8:

1. Specific positive reinforcement—whenever a coach positively reinforces a single player (e.g., "Nice catch, Sally").

2. General positive reinforcement—whenever a coach positively reinforces the team (e.g., "Good hustle out there").

3. Specific negative reinforcement—whenever a coach negatively reinforces a single player (e.g., "That was a poor pass, Jim").

4. General negative reinforcement—whenever a coach negatively reinforces the team (e.g., "Come on, that was poor execution").

5. Specific technical instruction—whenever a coach instructs a player (e.g., "Use two hands to catch the ball").

6. General technical instruction—whenever a coach instructs the team (e.g., "Let's play that zone defense a little tighter").

7. Keeping control—whenever the coach has to correct misbehavior or other breaches of discipline, other than game-related behavior (e.g., "Alright guys, let's pay attention").

8. Organization—whenever the coach instructs players for organizational chores (e.g., "Let's pick up all the bats here").

Using these categories, your job is to observe a coach and tally the number of times each behavior occurs. For the actual observation, use the Social Reinforcement Data Sheet.

To use the data sheet effectively, you will need to practice with the coding scheme for at least 30 minutes before you use it in the coaching setting. Observing the teaching of a physical education class is a good way to practice with the coding scheme.

You need to become familiar enough with each category to recognize the behavior and immediately code it in the appropriate spot. If you have to deliberate on a behavior, you may lose other behaviors.

Follow the steps listed here to conduct your observation.

Step 1. Select a children's organized sport that you can observe.

Step 2. With one other person from your class, go to a practice session. You should each have practiced for at least 30 minutes with the category system before you observe the game.

Step 3. Both of you (observers) view the practice and record the coach's comments on the Social Reinforcement Data Sheet. Each of you record your information separately. To facilitate this independent recording, ensure that the two of you are at least 10 feet apart while recording. Be sure that the situation you select allows both of you to see and hear the coach clearly, yet allows you to remain unobtrusive. If the coach asks you what you are doing, inform him or her fully. As a matter of interest, this is one learning experience for which you do not have to ask the coach for permission to observe. Coaching such sports is regarded as a public activity.

Step 4. Observe the coach for 45 minutes. Note each communication of the coach over the 45 minutes and categorize it as accurately as you can.

Analysis of Results

1. Total the behaviors in each category.
2. Calculate a ratio of positive to negative reinforcement.

   Number of positive reinforcements / Number of negative reinforcements

If the ratio is higher than 1, the coach used more positive reinforcement than negative reinforcement. The higher the ratio, the more positive a reinforcing agent the coach is. Obviously, with children, that is an important issue.

3. Other ratios that you could calculate to help you understand the coach's pattern of reinforcements include the following:

   Number of positive reinforcements / Total number of communications

   Number of negative reinforcements / Total number of communications

   Number of technical instructions / Total number of communications

   Number of specific positive reinforcements / Number of total positive reinforcements

   Number of specific negative reinforcements / Number of total negative reinforcements

Discussion Questions

Each ratio addresses a different issue in social reinforcement. For example, the ratio that deals with the number of positive reinforcers over the total number of communications indicates the commitment of the coach to positive reinforcement.

1. How did these ratios help you interpret the reinforcement philosophy of the coach?
2. In this experience, two of you observed the same coach for 45 minutes. How reliable were your results when compared with those of the other observer? For example, how did your total for specific positive reinforcement compare to your partner's total? What about comparisons for the other seven categories? Discuss any large differences that occurred. What should you do if large differences occurred?
3. What was the most frequent behavior? Why do you think it was the most frequent?

4.   If you thought the coach was an effective coach, what behaviors seemed to make him or her effective? Use your ratios to support your answer.

5.   What would you do in a teaching situation in terms of social reinforcement?

6.   How important is it to be specific in providing reinforcement in a teaching situation? What did you learn from the coach you observed in terms using specific reinforcement?

References

Black, S.J., & Weiss, M.R. (1992). The relationship among perceived coaching behaviors, perception of ability, and motivation in competitive age-group swimmers. *Journal of Sport & Exercise Psychology, 14,* 309-325.

Horn, T.S. (1992). Leadership effectiveness in the sport domain. In T.S. Horn (Ed.), *Advances in sport psychology* (pp. 181-200). Champaign, IL: Human Kinetics.

Kirschenbaum, D.S., & Smith, R.J. (1983). A preliminary study of sequencing effects in simulated coach feedback. *Journal of Sport Psychology, 5,* 332-342.

Petruzzello, S.J., & Corbin, C.B. (1988). The effects of performance feedback on female self-confidence. *Journal of Sport & Exercise Psychology, 10,* 174-183.

Smith, R.E., Smoll, F.L., Hunt, E., Curtis, B., & Coppel, D.B. (1979). Psychology and the bad news bears. In G.C. Roberts & K.M. Newell (Eds.), *Psychology of motor behavior and sport—1978* (pp. 109-130). Champaign, IL: Human Kinetics.

Solomon, G.B., Striegel, D.A., Eliot, J.F., Heon, S.N., Maas, J.L, & Wayda, V.K. (1996). The self-fulfilling prophecy in college basketball: Implications for effective coaching. *Journal of Applied Sport Psychology, 8,* 44-59.

Spink, K.S. (1988). The effects of modifying football on coaching behaviors. *Sports Coach, 11,* 19-24.

Vallerand, R.J. (1983). The effects of differential amounts of positive verbal feedback on the intrinsic motivation of male hockey players. *Journal of Sport Psychology, 5,* 100-107.

Weinberg, R.S., & Gould, D. (1995). *Foundations of sport and exercise psychology.* Champaign, IL: Human Kinetics.

Social Reinforcement Data Sheet

Name of observer _____

Sport _____

Category	Tally each occurrence	Total
Specific positive reinforcement		
General positive reinforcement		
Specific negative reinforcement		
General negative reinforcement		
Specific technical instruction		
General technical instruction		
Keeping control		
Organization		

EXPERIENCE 8

OBSERVATIONAL LEARNING

If you were asked to teach someone a new skill, what would be one of the first things you would do? Most teachers and coaches would give a physical demonstration of the skill. In fact, demonstration is the most widely used technique in teaching a new skill. When an individual acquires new forms of behavior merely by observing someone else (called a model), that individual is participating in *observational learning*.

Objectives

In this learning experience you will learn

- the psychological basis of the observational learning process;
- the effects of modeling correct responses;
- that characteristics of the model, such as status level, affect the learning that occurs; and
- the influence of developmental factors in the modeling process.

Then you will have the opportunity to assess the effectiveness of filmed demonstrations in the learning experience.

Basic Considerations

Observational learning occurs when an individual observes a model (live or on film) performing an act (e.g., motor or verbal) and approximates the act to learn that behavior. As an example, a young tennis player who watches his or her coach hit a topspin serve, then tries to repeat the action is involved in observational learning.

Although there are several theories available to explain how observational learning works, Bandura's (1986) social cognitive theory underpins most studies in the motor performance domain. Bandura has studied the process of observational learning for years. He posits that observational learning is determined by four subprocesses—attention, retention, motoric reproduction, and motivation (Bandura, 1986). According to Bandura, the attentional and retentional subprocesses influence skill acquisition, whereas the motoric reproduction and motivational subprocesses influence skill performance. The specifics of each subprocess are as follows:

1. **Attention.** It is clear that observers will fail to acquire the model's behavior unless they attend to and observe it carefully. Factors influencing the observer's attention include characteristics of the model (e.g., competence, status) and characteristics of the observer (e.g., age). A learner is more likely to attend to the demonstration performed by a highly competent, professional athlete, for example, than a demonstration by an unknown individual. Similarly, younger children are more likely to attend to a model who verbalizes important skill components than to a silent model who simply demonstrates the skill (Meaney, 1994).

2. **Retention.** The extent to which the observer recalls the model's behavior after observing the performance is influenced by symbolic coding. The greater the degree to which the observer can code the model's behavior, verbally or in vivid visual images, the greater the probability of recalling the behavior later. Evidence supporting the importance of symbolic coding in observational learning has been demonstrated (Weiss & Klint, 1987).

3. **Motoric reproduction.** Motor factors play an important role in observational learning. Quite simply, the observer must have the necessary motoric capabilities to reproduce the observed skill. If these physical responses are lacking, the motoric reproduction of the model's behavior will be retarded. An observer who symbolically codes the model's behavior may sometimes be unable to imitate it because of an existing physical limitation. A 6-year old boy, for example, is unlikely to be able to physically imitate the modeling of a shot put using a 16-lb shot.

4. **Motivation.** Motivational factors are important because they often determine whether the acquired responses will be translated into imitative behavior. Behaviors acquired and retained through observational learning will be activated into performance only when the observers are motivated, whether for intrinsic or extrinsic reasons.

Now that we have outlined the theory, what do we know about observational learning in sport contexts? Unfortunately, not much. Theories such as the one provided by Bandura (1986) give insight into basic questions, but little systematic investigation has been conducted. However, the available research does allow us to make some generalizations. First, modeling is effective for teaching complex tasks involving sequentially performed motor responses such as gymnastic routines or running basketball skills. Second, modeling correct responses is more desirable for learning than modeling incorrect responses. Martens, Burwitz, and Zuckerman (1976) provided support for both of these generalizations. They found that individuals performed a complex task better after observing the task modeled correctly or after observing a model first demonstrate incorrectly then correctly than they did after observing the task modeled incorrectly or after the modeling of an irrelevant task. Lirgg and Feltz (1991) found that individuals watching a skilled model performed better than those who watched an unskilled model.

Third, there is evidence to suggest that the status of the model will affect the amount of learning that occurs. McCullagh (1986) found that a high-status model was better than a low-status model. Fourth, evidence suggests that the social characteristics of the model influence the modeling process. For instance, both

McCullagh (1987) and George, Feltz, and Chase (1992) found that individuals who observed a model similar to themselves performed better than did individuals who observed a dissimilar model.

Fifth, developmental factors are important in the modelling process (McCullagh, Weiss, & Ross, 1989; Weiss, 1983). Weiss (1983) found that older children performed equally well after observing either a silent or a verbal model, but younger children performed better following a verbal model. She suggested that these differences reflected developmental factors such as attentional, retentional, and verbal-cognitive abilities. Sixth, both live and filmed models enhance an individual's self-efficacy beliefs in completing a required motor performance task (George et al., 1992; Lirgg & Feltz, 1991). In the Lirgg and Feltz (1991) study, for instance, they found higher self-efficacy levels reported by individuals who watched a skilled model than those who viewed an unskilled model.

Although these findings provide us with basic information about observational learning, many questions remain unanswered. As a result, teaching practices using demonstration techniques often are based on experience or intuition rather than on research evidence. We need much more systematic research to learn how to use demonstration more effectively. We designed the learning experience to sensitize you to the effectiveness of demonstrations on film and to the lack of widely accepted principles for their production.

Learning Experience

Purpose

To compare and contrast the effectiveness of two filmed demonstrations.

Measuring Tools

Two commercially produced videos demonstrating motor skills, obtained from your library department, and the Observational Learning Data Sheet on page 84.

Procedure

1. With four other persons from your class, select two videos demonstrating motor skills of comparable difficulty. As an example, you could compare a video demonstrating an advanced gymnastic skill such as a Tsukahara vault with an advanced diving trick such as a 2 1/2 reverse with pike. Alternatively, you could compare two simpler skills (i.e., a surface dive in swimming and a forehand stroke in tennis). Another possibility is comparing a video demonstrating atennis serve with a video demonstrating a jump shot in basketball.

2. View each video twice.

3. On the second viewing, all individuals should independently fill out the Observational Learning Data Sheet for each skill. The data sheet requires the observer to describe the activity, name the specific skill, categorize the model, then answer the questions by circling the number that best corresponds to his or her evaluation of the demonstration.

Analysis of Results

1. Obtain a mean for each question for both videos.
2. Compare the two videos in terms of the means for each question.

Discussion Questions

1. How effective was the first video in demonstrating the skills? How effective was the second video?
2. Which video was more effective? Why did you think so? Use the means you obtained to defend your answer.
3. How effective were the videos in getting your attention? Explain your answer.
4. How could the videos be more effective as a demonstration?
5. Were there any major differences in mean scores for the two videos? If so, why do you think that was?
6. What is the value of showing filmed skilled demonstrations to classes? Would you show the videos you viewed to a class you were teaching? Why or why not?

References

Bandura, A. (1986). *Social foundations of thought and action: A social cognitive theory*. Englewood Cliffs, NJ: Prentice Hall.

George, T.R., Feltz, D.L., & Chase, M.A. (1992). Effects of model similarity on self-efficacy and muscular endurance: A second look. *Journal of Sport & Exercise Psychology, 14*, 237-248.

Lirgg, C.D., & Feltz, D.L. (1991). Teacher versus peer models revisited: Effects on a motor performance and self-efficacy. *Research Quarterly for Exercise and Sport, 62*, 217-224.

Martens, R., Burwitz, L., & Zuckerman, J. (1976). Modelling effects on motor performance. *Research Quarterly, 47*, 277-291.

McCullagh, P. (1986). Model status as a determinant of observational learning and performance. *Journal of Sport Psychology, 8*, 319-331.

McCullagh, P. (1987). Model similarity effects on motor performance. *Journal of Sport Psychology, 9*, 249-260.

McCullagh, P., Weiss, M.R., & Ross, D. (1989). Modeling considerations in motor skill acquisition and performance: An integrated approach. In K.B. Pandolf (Ed.), *Exercise and sport sciences reviews* (pp. 475-513). Baltimore: Williams & Wilkins.

Meaney, K.S. (1994). Developmental modeling effects on the acquisition, retention, and transfer of a novel motor task. *Research Quarterly for Exercise and Sport, 65*, 31-39.

Weiss, M.R. (1983). Modelling and motor performance. A developmental perspective. *Research Quarterly for Exercise and Sport, 54*, 190-197.

Weiss, M.R., & Klint, K.A. (1987). "Show and Tell" in the gymnasium: An investigation of developmental differences in modeling and verbal rehearsal of motor skills. *Research Quarterly for Exercise and Sport, 58*, 234-241.

Observational Learning Data Sheet

Video 1

Activity _____

Specific skill(s) modeled _____

Who was the model (peer, expert, well-known personality)? _____

Answer the following questions by circling the number that corresponds to your opinion.

1. How complex was the skill?

    Simple   **Complex**
    1   **2**   **3**   **4**   **5**   **6**   **7**

2. How well did the model demonstrate the skills?

    Very well   **Very poorly**
    1   **2**   **3**   **4**   **5**   **6**   **7**

3. How effective was the video as a demonstration?

    Very ineffective   **Very effective**
    1   **2**   **3**   **4**   **5**   **6**   **7**

4. How effective was the video as a motivating aid?

    Very ineffective   **Very effective**
    1   **2**   **3**   **4**   **5**   **6**   **7**

Video 2

Activity _____

Specific skill(s) modeled _____

Who was the model (peer, expert, well-known personality)? _____

Answer the following questions by circling the number that corresponds to your opinion.

1.   How complex was the skill?

   Simple   **Complex**
       1   **2**   **3**   **4**   **5**   **6**   **7**

2.   How well did the model demonstrate the skills?

   Very well   **Very poorly**
       1   **2**   **3**   **4**   **5**   **6**   **7**

3.   How effective was the video as a demonstration?

   Very ineffective   **Very effective**
       1   **2**   **3**   **4**   **5**   **6**   **7**

4.   How effective was the video as a motivating aid?

   Very ineffective   **Very effective**
       1   **2**   **3**   **4**   **5**   **6**   **7**

EXPERIENCE 9

ANXIETY

You have no doubt seen athletes perform poorly because they were uptight and anxious, and you may have experienced this yourself. Anxiety is manifested as feeling apprehensive and uncertain and experiencing physical symptoms such as butterflies in the stomach, sweaty palms, and a thumping heart. The more important the competition, the more likely you will experience these anxiety symptoms. The tendency for individuals to become anxious in sport has prompted investigators to identify sources of anxiety and to learn how different individuals perceive them.

Objectives

In this learning experience you will learn

- the differences among the terms arousal, stress, and anxiety;
- the definition of trait anxiety and state anxiety;
- the definition of somatic and cognitive anxiety; and
- the relationship between arousal or anxiety and performance.

Then you will have the opportunity to find the state anxiety of individuals who are about to compete in a hypothetical contest and correlate the state anxiety with their trait anxiety.

Basic Considerations

Three terms that have been used interchangeably over the years, but have important theoretical distinctions are arousal, stress, and anxiety. These terms require clarification. Historically, *arousal* has been viewed as physiological activation that runs on a continuum from deep sleep to extreme excitement. In recent years, this activation has been extended to include a cognitive or mental intensity of behavior as well. Combining these two ideas, Gould and Krane have defined arousal as "general physiological and psychological activation of the organism that varies on a continuum from deep sleep to intense excitement" (1992, pp.120-121).

Stress, on the other hand, occurs when a large imbalance exists between what individuals perceive is required in a given situation and what they feel their capabilities are, when they believe the outcome is important (McGrath, 1970). For example, a hockey player awarded a penalty shot who realizes that if it goes in, it will win the championship game, but who hasn't scored all year is likely to perceive an imbalance in what is required, and thus feel stressed.

The term *anxiety,* which differs from the preceding two terms, has several important distinctions. One early distinction concerned whether anxiety referred to a tendency to be anxious or to an immediate anxiety state associated with a situation. This difference was captured in terms of Spielberger's trait-state distinction. Spielberger (1966) defined state anxiety as an existing or immediate emotional state character-ized by apprehension and tension. Trait anxiety was defined as a predisposition to perceive certain situations as threatening and to respond to them with varying levels of state anxiety.

Both state and trait anxiety have been further subdivided into cognitive and somatic anxiety. According to Martens, Vealey, and Burton (1990), cognitive anxiety is the mental component of anxiety and is caused by negative performance evaluations, whereas somatic anxiety is the physiological and affective elements of the anxiety experience that relate to autonomic arousal. Manifestations of somatic anxiety would include things such as butterflies in the stomach, sweaty palms, muscle tension, elevated heart rate, and shortness of breath.

Although general measures of both trait and state anxiety are available, the most promising avenue of research in sport has assumed that anxiety is situation specific, rather than a global measure that pervades all situations. Using this approach, Martens (1977) developed an instrument, titled the Sport Competition Anxiety Test (SCAT), specifically to measure competitive trait anxiety. Researchers using this sport-specific measure have found it to be a better predictor in the sport setting than general measures. Although SCAT has been useful in assessing competitive trait anxiety, one of its drawbacks is that it views trait anxiety as unidimensional. Newer instruments have now been developed to assess cognitive and somatic trait anxiety in the sport setting (Smith, Smoll, & Schutz, 1990).

A sport-specific inventory that measures the multidimensional nature of state anxiety also has been developed. Called the Competitive State Anxiety Inventory-2 (CSAI-2), the scale assesses the cognitive and somatic components of state anxiety (Martens, Vealey, & Burton, 1990). Since its development, it has received wide-spread use in the assessment of state anxiety within the competitive sport setting.

The development of these sport-specific anxiety instruments has allowed re-searchers to investigate an important issue—the effect of arousal or anxiety on athletic performance. Researchers have proposed several explanations, both theo-retical and empirical, for the relationship between arousal or anxiety and perfor-mance. Two of the oldest explanations, drive theory and the Inverted-U hypothesis, attempt to relate arousal to performance. Although drive theory and the Inverted-U have received support over the years, both are now seen as too simplistic to explain the relationship between arousal and performance (Krane, 1993).

More recent explanations have focused on the relationship between anxiety and performance. One explanation considers the multidimensional nature of state anxiety, hence its name—the multidimensional theory of state anxiety (Martens, Vealey, & Burton, 1990). The main premise of this theory is that cognitive and somatic anxiety will have different effects on athletic performance. Specifically, they predict that cognitive anxiety will have a negative linear relationship with performance, whereas somatic anxiety will be related to performance in an Inverted-U manner. Further, they believe that somatic anxiety should influence performance less than cognitive anxiety, unless somatic anxiety becomes so great that it diverts attention from the task at hand (Martens, Vealey, & Burton, 1990). Although the predictions from the theory have intuitive appeal, recent research has not provided clear support for its predictions (Hardy, 1996). Krane (1992) has suggested that these inconsistencies might be resolved by examining the combined effects of cognitive and somatic anxiety, rather than treating these two anxiety subcomponents as independent, as past research has done. One new theory that attempts to do this is catastrophe theory.

Catastrophe theory (Hardy, 1996) was developed to explain the interaction between cognitive and somatic anxiety and their combined relationship with athletic performance. It is worth pointing out that although we use the term somatic anxiety here, researchers differ on whether this should be somatic anxiety (Krane, 1992) or simply physiological arousal (Hardy, 1996) that is assessed along with cognitive anxiety. Predictions from catastrophe theory suggest that performance is associated with increases in somatic anxiety to some optimal level. However, differing from other theories, it also suggests that the effects of somatic anxiety may interact with cognitive anxiety to differentially influence performance. Specifically, it predicts that performance will be fine as long as cognitive anxiety remains low. However, when high somatic anxiety combines with high levels of cognitive anxiety, it predicts a rapid decline in performance (i.e., a catastrophic effect). This somatic anxiety can have different effects on performance, depending on the amount of cognitive anxiety the athlete is experiencing. Consistent with other theoretical explanations, it predicts a negative linear relationship between cognitive anxiety and performance. The few studies that have addressed the theoretical predictions of the model have found initial support (Hardy, 1996).

A final model we will present here that addresses the relationship between arousal or anxiety and performance is called the ZOF (zone of optimal functioning) model. In this model it has been suggested that each individual has a unique pregame zone of anxiety at which performance is facilitated (Hanin, 1980). Specifically, each athlete is seen to have a specific band of anxiety in which best performances will most likely occur. This band of anxiety is known as the zone of optimal functioning (ZOF). Although the hypothesis is still new, recent research has found increasing support for the ZOF explanation. That is, athletes' best performances occur when cognitive and somatic anxiety fall within their zones of optimal functioning. Conversely, poor performances occur when both types of anxiety fall outside the athletes' zones of optimal functioning (Krane, 1993).

There have been great strides made in recent years explaining the anxiety and performance relationship. Although the much quoted Inverted-U hypothesis has served us well in the past, it is now time to move to more comprehensive theories explaining how anxiety impacts athletic performance. The move to multidimensional sport anxiety research should result in exciting and important findings in the years to come. The learning experience offers you an opportunity to investigate multidimensional anxiety levels using the CSAI-2 inventory.

Learning Experience

Purpose

To investigate anxiety levels in a sport situation using the SCAT and CSAI-2 inventories.

Measuring Tools

The trait measure of SCAT (labeled as the Illinois Competition Questionnaire) on page 92, the state measure of CSAI-2 (labeled as the Illinois Self-Evaluation Questionnaire) on page 94 and the Anxiety Data Sheet on page 96.

Procedure

1. Select 10 or more individuals (age 15 or older) who regularly participate in organized sport (e.g., varsity or intramural). These may be individuals in your dormitory, fraternity, sorority, or other group.

2. Administer the SCAT inventory (Illinois Competitive Questionnaire) to each of them. This is a trait-anxiety score.

3. Have participants read the following sport question; then have them complete the CSAI-2 to obtain a state-anxiety score for this situation:

> Remember the last championship game that you played in and lost. Think about how you felt waiting to start that game (5 minutes before game time). Use the questionnaire (CSAI-2) to record your feelings.

Analysis of Results

Determine the SCAT score using these directions.

1. Score items 2, 3, 5, 8, 9, 12, 14, and 15 as follows:
   1—hardly ever
   2—sometimes
   3—often

2. Score items 6 and 11 as follows:
   1—often
   2—sometimes
   3—hardly ever

3. Do not score items 1, 4, 7, 10, and 13. These are dummy variables and are used often on questionnaires such as this to disguise the questionnaire.

4. Add the scores. Scores range from 10 (low competitive trait anxiety) to 30 (high competitive trait anxiety).

Determine the CSAI-2 score using the following directions:

5. The CSAI-2 has three subscales—cognitive anxiety, somatic anxiety, and self-confidence. Score each separately as follows:

   i. Cognitive state anxiety. Total the scores to items 1, 4, 7, 10, 13, 16, 19, 22, and 25.

    ii.   Somatic state anxiety. Total the scores to items 2, 5, 8, 11, 14, 17, 20, 23, and 26. Use reverse scoring for item 14 (1 = 4, 2 = 3, 3 = 2, 4 = 1) before adding it to the total score.

    iii.   State self-confidence. Total the scores to items 3, 6, 9, 12, 15, 18, 21, 24, and 27.

6.   Add the scores for each subscale. Scores range from a low of 9 to a high of 36. The higher the score for each subscale, the greater the cognitive anxiety, the somatic anxiety, and the level of state self-confidence.

7.   Number your participants from 1 to 10 (or more), and use the Anxiety Data Sheet to correlate the scores from SCAT and the two state-anxiety scores (cognitive and somatic) from the CSAI-2. (See page 37 for an example of how to set up the table to compute a Pearson product-moment correlation on the data.)

8.   Compute two correlations.

    i. SCAT and cognitive state anxiety.

    ii. SCAT and somatic state anxiety.

Discussion Questions

1.   What is the meaning of the correlation coefficients obtained? Are the correlations high or low?

2.   Is SCAT a good predictor of pregame cognitive state anxiety?

3.   Is SCAT a good predictor of pregame somatic state anxiety?

4.   Is SCAT a better predictor of state cognitive or somatic anxiety?

5.   What is the role of the coach in trying to control the state anxiety of players?

6.   If the players are already anxious, what should the coach do in a pregame talk?

References

Gould, D., & Krane, V. (1992). The arousal-athletic performance relationship: Current status and future directions. In T.S. Horn (Ed.), *Advances in sport psychology* (pp. 119-141). Champaign, IL: Human Kinetics.

Hanin, Y.L. (1980). A study of anxiety in sport. In W.F. Straub (Ed.), *Sport psychology: An analysis of athlete behavior* (pp. 236-249). Ithaca, NY: Mouvement.

Hardy, L. (1996). Testing the predictions of the Cusp catastrophe model of anxiety and performance. *The Sport Psychologist, 10,* 140-156.

Krane, V. (1992). Conceptual and methodological considerations in sport anxiety research: From the Inverted-U hypothesis to catastrophe theory. *Quest, 44,* 72-87.

Krane, V. (1993). A practical application of the anxiety-athletic performance relationship: The Zone of Optimal Functioning hypothesis. *The Sport Psychologist, 7,* 113-126.

Martens, R. (1977). *Sport Competition Anxiety Test.* Champaign, IL: Human Kinetics.

Martens, R., Vealey, R.S., & Burton, D. (1990). *Competitive anxiety in sport.* Champaign, IL: Human Kinetics.

McGrath, J.E. (1970). Major methodological issues. In J.E. McGrath (Ed.), *Social and psychological factors in stress* (pp. 19-49). New York: Holt, Rinehart & Winston.

Smith, R.E., Smoll, E.L., & Schutz, R.W. (1990). Measurement and correlates of sport-specific cognitive and somatic anxiety: The Sport Anxiety Scale. *Anxiety Research, 2,* 263-280.

Spielberger, C. (Ed.) (1966). *Anxiety and behavior.* New York: Academic Press.

Illinois Competition Questionnaire

Below are some statements about how individuals feel when they compete in sports and games. Read each statement and decide if you hardly ever, sometimes, or often feel this way when you compete. There are no right or wrong answers. Do not spend too much time on any one statement. Remember to choose the word that describes how you usually feel when competing in sports and games.

1. Competing against others is socially enjoyable.

Hardly ever	**Sometimes**	**Often**
1	2	3

2. Before I compete I feel uneasy.

Hardly ever	**Sometimes**	**Often**
1	2	3

3. Before I compete I worry about not performing well.

Hardly ever	**Sometimes**	**Often**
1	2	3

4. I am a good sport when I compete.

Hardly ever	**Sometimes**	**Often**
1	2	3

5. When I compete I worry about making mistakes.

Hardly ever	**Sometimes**	**Often**
1	2	3

6. Before I compete I am calm.

Hardly ever	**Sometimes**	**Often**
1	2	3

7.   Setting a goal is important when competing.

Hardly ever	**Sometimes**	**Often**
1	2	3

8.   Before I compete I get a queasy feeling in my stomach.

Hardly ever	**Sometimes**	**Often**
1	2	3

9.   Just before competition I notice my heart beats faster than usual.

Hardly ever	**Sometimes**	**Often**
1	2	3

10.   I like to compete in games that demand considerable physical energy.

Hardly ever	**Sometimes**	**Often**
1	2	3

11.   Before I compete I feel relaxed.

Hardly ever	**Sometimes**	**Often**
1	2	3

12.   Before I compete I am nervous.

Hardly ever	**Sometimes**	**Often**
1	2	3

13.   Team sports are more exciting than individual sports.

Hardly ever	**Sometimes**	**Often**
1	2	3

14.   I get nervous waiting to start the game.

Hardly ever	**Sometimes**	**Often**
1	2	3

15.   Before I compete I usually get uptight.

Hardly ever	**Sometimes**	**Often**
1	2	3

Illinois Self-Evaluation Questionnaire

A number of statements that athletes have used to describe their feelings before competition are given here. Read each statement, then circle the appropriate number to the right of the statement to indicate how you felt 5 minutes before that championship. There are no right or wrong answers. Do not spend too much time on any one statement, but choose the answer that describes your feelings 5 minutes before that championship.

	Not at all	Some-what	Moderately so	Very much so
1. I am concerned about this competition.	1	2	3	4
2. I feel nervous.	1	2	3	4
3. I feel at ease.	1	2	3	4
4. I have self-doubts.	1	2	3	4
5. I feel jittery.	1	2	3	4
6. I feel comfortable.	1	2	3	4
7. I am concerned that I may not do as well in this competition as I could.	1	2	3	4
8. My body feels tense.	1	2	3	4
9. I feel self-confident.	1	2	3	4
10. I am concerned about losing.	1	2	3	4
11. I feel tense in my stomach.	1	2	3	4
12. I feel secure.	1	2	3	4
13. I am concerned about choking under pressure.	1	2	3	4
14. My body feels relaxed.	1	2	3	4
15. I'm confident I can meet the challenge.	1	2	3	4
16. I'm concerned about performing poorly.	1	2	3	4
17. My heart is racing.	1	2	3	4
18. I'm confident about performing well.	1	2	3	4
19. I'm concerned about reaching my goal.	1	2	3	4
20. I feel my stomach sinking.	1	2	3	4

	Not at all	Some-what	Moderately so	Very much so
21. I feel mentally relaxed.	1	2	3	4
22. I'm concerned that others will be disappointed with my performance.	1	2	3	4
23. My hands are clammy.	1	2	3	4
24. I'm confident because I mentally picture myself reaching my goal.	1	2	3	4
25. I'm concerned I won't be able to concentrate.	1	2	3	4
26. My body feels tight.	1	2	3	4
27. I'm confident of coming through under pressure.	1	2	3	4

Anxiety Data Sheet

Subjects	SCAT (x)	CSAI-2 Som y_1	CSAI-2 Cog y_2	x	y_1	y_2	x^2	y_1^2	y_2^2	xy_1	xy_2
1.											
2.											
3.											
4.											
5.											
6.											
7.											
8.											
9.											
10.											
							Σx^2	Σy_1^2	Σy_2^2	Σxy_1	Σxy_2

$\Sigma x^2 =$

$\Sigma y_1^2 =$

$\Sigma y_2^2 =$

$\Sigma xy_1 =$

$\Sigma xy_2 =$

SCAT/Som

$$r = \frac{\Sigma xy_1}{\sqrt{\left(\Sigma x^2\right)\left(\Sigma y_1{}^2\right)}}$$

SCAT/Cog

$$r = \frac{\Sigma xy_2}{\sqrt{\left(\Sigma x^2\right)\left(\Sigma y_2{}^2\right)}}$$

EXPERIENCE 10

AGGRESSION

You need only read the newspaper or watch the news to realize that violence and aggression permeate our society. Aggression aimed at our fellow humans is legion and has been noted in contexts ranging from wars between nations to rivalry between young children. Acts of aggression in sport also are rampant. The newspapers report incidents in which coaches encourage athletes to physically hurt opposing athletes, and athletes have ended up in criminal court as a result of their conduct during games. As we can appreciate, aggression in sport is a source of real concern for sport program administrators.

Objectives

In this learning experience you will learn

- the definition of aggression,
- the theories concerned with why humans aggress against their fellow humans, and
- the relationship between competition and aggression.

Then you will have the opportunity to observe and analyze acts of aggression that occur during a professional sporting encounter.

Basic Considerations

Aggression is a term used in many contexts in society. For instance, in the business community, you often hear about companies wishing to hire aggressive sales people. In this context, aggressive refers to ambitious people who are highly driven to attain goals. In the sporting context, you hear about Greg Norman's aggressive golf style, about aggressive net play in tennis, or about aggressive rebounding in basketball. Although these examples imply that aggressive behavior is positive, from a scientific perspective, the term aggression describes something very different.

From a scientific perspective, Baron (1977) has defined aggression as any form of behavior directed toward harming or injuring another living being. Embedded within this scientific definition are four distinguishing characteristics:

1. It is a behavior. A hockey player who thinks about popping an opponent in the head with his fist is not being aggressive. A behavior must occur.

2. There must be intention. The basketball player fighting for a rebound who breaks an opponent's jaw when he swings his elbow for position is not being aggressive. The player must intend to inflict harm or injury to classify this act as aggression. As another example, if a football player goes all out to tackle a quarterback and tackles hard to prevent him throwing the ball, that is not an act of aggression, no matter how vigorous or motivated the player. Even if the quarterback incurs an injury, it is accidental and part of the game. Many coaches and spectators often call this type of behavior aggressive; from a scientific perspective, however, it is not. This type of purposeful, goal-directed behavior in which there is no intent to harm has been labeled assertive behavior (Husman & Silva, 1984). If, on the other hand, the player deliberately hurts the quarterback to get him out of the game (by going for his head or spearing him with a helmet), that is aggression. Intent to injure is usually determined by the referee, but his or her interpretation is not infallible.

3. It must involve harm or injury. Further, this act can be either physical (e.g., hitting an opponent across the arm with your hockey stick) or psychological (e.g., saying something hurtful to another player with the intent to diminish respect for the player).

4. It involves living beings. A hockey coach who breaks a stick over the boards after the referee makes a bad call or a basketball coach who throws a chair onto the court after a bad call are not being aggressive. The act must be directed toward a living organism for it to be aggression.

Within the general category of aggression, we make further distinctions about the type of aggressive behavior being carried out. The two types of aggressive behavior often identified are instrumental and hostile aggression (Husman & Silva, 1984). Instrumental aggression is aggressive behavior carried out to achieve nonaggressive goals, whereas hostile or reactive aggression has harm or injury to another person as the primary goal. The soccer player who, in attempting to stop a goal, breaks an opponent's leg with a hard tackle is engaging in instrumental aggression. On the other hand, the player who breaks another player's nose with a punch after the whistle has blown and play has stopped is likely engaging in hostile aggression.

Theories of Aggression

Because of the pervasiveness of violence and aggression in our society, considerable research has been devoted to understanding why aggression occurs. This empirical research, focusing on the origin, instigation, and maintenance of aggression, has substantially increased the understanding of many processes mediating aggression, but we have yet to derive a sufficient explanation of why humans aggress against their fellow humans. However, researchers have forwarded several theories about acts of aggression.

The oldest theoretical position states that aggression is instinctual. The instinct view of aggression has received much impetus from ethologists, such as Lorenz. Lorenz (1966) believed that aggression builds up within an individual and this buildup needs some form of release. The release may occur through either an acceptable or an unacceptable (antisocial) act. Sport would serve as a suitable vehicle, for example, whereas war would not. In fact, Lorenz advocates that sport ought to be a substitute for war. In other words, because all competitive sport situations hold some degree of conflict between opponents, participation in them allows individuals to dissipate aggression in an acceptable manner. The process through which aggression is dissipated is termed *catharsis*. Thus, if someone displaces his or her aggression by going out and hurting or injuring an opponent because it makes them feel better, then this is a cathartic act.

Another popular conception is that aggression is a reaction to frustrating experiences. This theory, called the frustration-aggression hypothesis, was initially proposed by Dollard, Miller, Doob, Mowrer, and Sears in 1939. The theory suggests that frustration, defined as the blocking of goal-directed behavior, creates a drive to aggress against a person. Through aggression, the drive is dissipated.

In recent years, another theoretical position regarding aggression has emerged. Based on the social learning theory of Bandura (1973), it focuses on aggression as learned social behavior. Bandura suggests two mechanisms whereby an individual acquires aggressive patterns of behavior. An individual may add aggressive responses to behavior through observational learning or through experiences in which he or she is rewarded for such behavior. The individual learns that aggression is not only permissible in certain situations but also useful for modifying a social situation in a direction consistent with his or her desire. To illustrate, a retaliatory act of aggression against an opponent that quells the opponent or a temper tantrum that enables a young player to get his or her way both reinforce the utilitarian power of aggression.

A final theory of aggression has been posited by Berkowitz (1969), who extended the work of Dollard et al. (1939). Berkowitz postulated that learning and innate sources of aggression coexist. Specifically, he suggested that frustration "prompts" an individual for aggression, but it is the cues in the environment that determine whether aggression occurs. For example, the hockey player who is frustrated because of an opponent's clutching and grabbing may not retaliate aggressively because the referee is watching, but may act aggressively toward the opponent in another situation when the referee is looking the other way.

Sport and Aggression

Given that aggression does occur in contact sports such as ice hockey and football, two possible explanations surface immediately. The first is that there must be some positive relationship between aggressive behavior and performance outcome in these sports. That is, teams use aggression to win games. Or, second, because frustration is an inherent part of sport, teams who do not achieve their goals (e.g., those who lose) exhibit high levels of aggression.

The evidence for the first explanation is equivocal. For instance, although Widmeyer and Birch (1984) found that NHL (National Hockey League) teams who were more aggressive early in a contest won more games, a study by McGuire, Courneya, Widmeyer, and Carron (1992) found no significant relationship. Thus, the relationship between success in ice hockey and increased aggression has yet to be established with any consistency.

Concerning the alternative explanation that the frustration inherent in sport may cause high levels of aggressive behavior in losing teams, the evidence also is inconsistent. For example, McGuire (1990) examined which team was winning and losing at the time of the aggressive act. He found no significant difference between these two groups, using NHL teams. However, other research with ice hockey teams has found that losing teams were more aggressive in the third period than winning teams (Widmeyer & Birch, 1984), and teams that were losing by more than three goals were more aggressive than teams losing by fewer goals (McGuire, 1990).

Another factor that may help to explain some instances of aggression in sport concerns the opponent's intent. Specifically, several studies have shown that the athlete who perceives an opponent trying to inflict harm or injury is more likely to respond with aggression against that opponent than if he or she perceives otherwise. Brice (1990), for example, using university ice hockey players, found that the biggest cause of wanting to hurt someone resulted from that individual previously injuring or attempting to injure him or a teammate.

As these studies illustrate, the explanation for aggression in sport is far from clear. Thus, the question remains: What causes aggression within a sporting environment? Possibly, aggression results from the fact that competition in itself is arousing. Alternatively, aggression may emanate from the fact that competition is frustrating because people anticipate defeat. A third possible reason may be the inherent provocation within the sporting situation that causes individuals to aggress.

It is reasonable to assume that aggression is a combination of several causes. Competition is arousing in itself, participation often increases the levels of arousal, and competitors in an aroused state frequently overreact to stimuli. Aggressive acts occur in sport in the heat of the moment because of some perceived provocation that may or may not be intended. Whatever the reason, we need more research on this topic.

The learning experience included here is designed to answer a simple, but important question: How much aggression occurs in competitive sport?

Learning Experience

Purpose

To determine the number of acts of aggression that occur in a professional sporting encounter (or other high-level contest, if you cannot view a professional contest).

Measuring Tool

Aggression Data Sheet on page 103.

Procedure

1. Select one contact sport contest to observe. Some suitable sports to observe include football, ice hockey, and basketball.

2. Observe the contest live if you can. Although it is acceptable to view the sport on television, we do not recommend this because your observation is limited to what the camera picks up and too much data can be lost.

3. Observe the entire game and record the aggressive acts on the Aggression Data Sheet. If you record fewer than three acts of aggression, observe another contest. Because aggression implies an intent to injure or hurt (accidental injury is not aggression), you may have to observe several contests to see three acts of aggression.

4. Interpret the antecedents of each aggressive act (i.e., frustration, retaliation, overarousal, provocation, no apparent reason) and briefly note the reason(s) on the data sheet.

5. Record the approximate time each act of aggression occurred.

6. Record the score at the time of the aggressive act.

Analysis of Results

1. Determine the factors that influenced the acts of aggression you observed. Did the following factors influence aggression?

   - Situational factors
   - Time of the game
   - Score (behind, ahead, by how much)

2. Compare your explanations with those of the rest of the class.

Discussion Questions

1. How many aggressive acts did you observe? Based on the results, would you suggest that sport is conducive to promoting aggression?

2. Did the acts of aggression cluster in time? For instance, did a majority of acts occur near the start of the game, the middle, or the end? If a pattern emerged, can you explain it?

3. Did the team behind in score exhibit more acts of aggression? If so, can you explain this with any theories put forward?

4. Were there any common antecedent conditions? For instance, did frustration seem to be an important antecedent of the aggression?

5. If you were a coach of a children's team, would you have them observe a game between teams that were notoriously aggressive? Use one of the theories to explain your answer.

References

Bandura, A. (1973). *Aggression: A social learning analysis.* Englewood Cliffs, NJ: Prentice Hall.

Baron, R.A. (1977). *Human aggression.* New York: Plenum Press.

Berkowitz, L. (1969). The frustration-aggression hypothesis revisited. In L. Berkowitz (Ed.), *Roots of aggression* (pp. 1-29). New York: Atherton Press.

Brice, J.D. (1990). *Frustration in ice hockey: Extent, antecedents, and consequences.* Unpublished master's thesis, University of Waterloo, Ontario, Canada.

Dollard, J., Miller, N., Doob, L., Mowrer, O., & Sears, R. (1939). *Frustration and aggression.* New Haven, CT: Yale University Press.

Husman, B.F., & Silva, J.M. (1984). Aggression in sport: Definitional and theoretical considerations. In J.M. Silva & R.S. Weinberg (Eds.), *Psychological foundations of sport* (pp. 246-260). Champaign, IL: Human Kinetics.

Lorenz, K. (1966). *On aggression.* New York: Harcourt, Brace and World.

McGuire, E.J. (1990). *The antecedents of aggressive behaviour in professional ice hockey.* Unpublished doctoral dissertation, University of Waterloo, Waterloo, Ontario, Canada.

McGuire, E.J., Courneya, K.S., Widmeyer, W.N., & Carron, A.V. (1992). Aggression as a potential mediator of the home advantage in professional ice hockey. *Journal of Sport & Exercise Psychology, 14,* 148-158.

Widmeyer, W.N., & Birch, J.S. (1984). Aggression in professional ice hockey: A strategy for success or a reaction to failure? *Journal of Psychology, 117,* 77-84.

Aggression Data Sheet

Activity _____

Live _____   Televised _____

Behavior	Antecedents	Time	Score
Aggressive[1]	Reasons aggression occurred		

[1]Aggressive behavior means an intent to injure or hurt. Accidental behavior is *not* aggression.

EXPERIENCE 11

UNDERSTANDING MOTIVATION

A central issue in sport psychology is motivation. An insight into how the construct of motivation functions in sport and physical activity settings is important to sport psychologists and has practical relevance for coaches, teachers, and parents. Why do some athletes train hard but others don't train as hard, despite what the coach and parents say? Why are some athletes more persistent? Why do some athletes drop out? Why do individuals play certain sports to the exclusion of others? These questions pertain to individual motivation. This learning experience examines some psychological processes underlying the motivation of individuals.

Objectives

In this learning experience you will learn

- two contemporary approaches to motivation,
- the social cognitive basis of motivation,
- some important issues in the area of causal attributions and motivation,
- the motivational implications of holding an achievement goal, and
- the process of motivation.

Then you will have the opportunity to do a research project in which you will conduct a field study to measure the achievement goals of athletes and look at the motivational implications of these goals.

Basic Considerations

This learning experience focuses on motivation as an individual difference variable. We assume that there are some thought processes affecting motivated behavior; however, we have to confess that there are many misunderstandings about the process of motivation. Many people confuse arousal with motivation, so that locker room talks are assumed to motivate athletes. Recently, Jackie Sherrill of Mississippi

State had a longhorn bull castrated midfield before the game when they were to play the Texas Longhorns as a means of motivating his team! Dale Christensen, the coach at Libertyville High School in Illinois, staged a fake shooting to make his players "combat ready" for a game. There are many bizarre tactics that well-meaning but misguided coaches have used to motivate individuals for sport competition. However, as we shall see, arousal is not motivation.

There are many approaches to the study of motivation, but in this learning experience we will concentrate on recent approaches. The older and more traditional approach assumes that individuals have a personality trait to achieve, and that this motivates them to perform. Much early research using this approach focused on identifying and measuring the motivation to achieve, and many scales were developed to this end. Unfortunately, these scales tended to correlate poorly, leading to the more recent emphasis on situation-specific scales. Once high or low motivation is identified, investigators focusing on predictions of behavior in certain situations have been remarkably successful (e.g., Atkinson & Feather, 1966). This line of research has been less successful, however, in identifying why or how individuals are motivated.

The contemporary approach focuses on why and how individuals are motivated and is the subject of this learning experience. It explores the cognitions individuals make in achievement-oriented situations such as sport competition. Humans are viewed as active, information-processing organisms, with thought the basis of action. Thoughts, or the beliefs that individuals have about the cause of events, or their perceived goal in the context are believed to determine their behavior. The focus of this avenue of research is to investigate these thoughts and determine how they affect achievement and motivated behavior.

The social cognitive approach is reflected in two contemporary motivation approaches. The first one is the body of research generated from *attribution theory*. Attribution theory focuses on the process of making cognitions relative to one's environment and on the implications of such inferences. Individuals attempt to understand the causes of past outcomes. By understanding these causes, usually called *causal attributions*, individuals gain a powerful prerequisite to effective action. As an example, an athlete who understands that a recent failure was a result of inadequate preparation can rectify the problem by better preparation.

The Attributional Approach

The study of causal attributions for success and failure has been shown by Weiner (1986) to have important implications for achievement-related behavior. Even though the attribution process is more complex, in general, success and failure have been attributed to factors within three dimensions: stability, locus of causality, and control. For simplicity, we shall deal only with stability and locus of causality. Individuals are assumed to attribute outcomes to one or more of four factors: ability, effort, task difficulty, and luck. The individual attempts to explain success or failure by assessing level of ability, the amount of effort expended, the difficulty of the task, and the type and amount of luck experienced. Of the four factors, ability and effort have an internal locus of control, whereas task difficulty and luck have an external locus of control. The degree to which an individual attributes success and failure to internal or external factors influences the degree of affect associated with the outcome—the amount of pride or shame experienced.

Ability and task difficulty are considered stable factors, whereas effort and luck are considered relatively unstable. Weiner et al. (1971) have shown that future expectations of performance are determined by the stability of the causal attributions. If failure is attributed to low ability, for example, the individual cannot expect to win in the future. Further, the stability dimension affects persistence. As an example, individuals who believe that they failed because of a lack of effort, an unstable causal factor, may try harder and persist longer in the future because they know effort is controllable. Thus, the attributions made following success or failure can influence motivation and determine future achievement behaviors.

The attributional process has obvious and important implications for sport situations. First, the causal attribution model has been successfully applied to the achievement-oriented sport situation (e.g., Spink, 1978). Second, winning and losing in sport contests are important to the participants. Thus, the study of causal attributions for winning and losing in athletic contests has potential for understanding motivated behavior in sport and physical education.

Individuals involved in sport make attributions based on the outcome of the activity. Winning is attributed to ability and effort, and losing is attributed to luck, task difficulty, and, in some cases, ability (Roberts, 1975; Spink, 1978). Although much early sport research used Weiner's four factors as the only reasons to explain outcomes, several studies have adopted an open-ended approach. The basic findings suggest that limiting an individual's attribution to the traditional causes outlined by Weiner is inadequate to explain sport outcomes (e.g., Roberts & Pascuzzi, 1979).

Roberts and Pascuzzi (1979), for example, found that the four traditional attributes were used only 45% of the time in explaining sport outcomes. In fact, they identified many additional factors. However, the important finding was that the dimensions identified by Weiner were important in the motivation equation. More recent research has used measurement instruments that identify the important dimensions for understanding motivation (e.g., McAuley & Duncan, 1990). We need more research to determine the full range of possible responses in a sport setting.

In sport research, individuals in sporting situations who consistently won or lost attributed the outcome to stable dimensions, particularly ability. In the case of consistent success, the attribution was to high ability, whereas in consistent failure, the attribution was to low ability. The implications are evident. Success experiences may lead the individual to associate the outcome of the activity with an internal and stable attribution (ability), so the individual tries harder to achieve higher performance levels. Conversely, consistent failure may lead individuals to believe that they have little ability, and they therefore exert little effort in similar future situations. These individuals may seek to avoid the activity and drop out altogether. It is these findings pertaining to ability that led to the proposal of another conceptual process explaining motivation. We shall discuss that process next.

Achievement Goals and Motivation

The framework that has become popular is a social cognitive approach derived from the achievement goal approach of Nicholls (1989). Nicholls focused on the goal-directed nature of achievement behavior and argued that the perception of ability is the distinguishing feature of achievement motivation. However, two conceptions of ability exist in achievement contexts. Thus, individuals approach tasks with one understanding of the meaning of ability, and this affects their perceptions and beliefs about the activity.

These two conceptions of ability are assumed to be invoked by either a dispositional, or "in the head" variable, or by the perceived situational demands.

Thus, an athlete is in one of two states of involvement, and we use the terms *task* and *ego* to identify these two states. An individual who is task involved focuses on developing skills, learning new skills, and demonstrating mastery at the task. The demonstration of ability is based on maximum effort and is self-referenced. In contrast, an individual who is ego involved focuses on being able with reference to others. The demonstration of ability is based on outperforming others with minimum effort. If the person is task involved, then perceived normative ability is not relevant, as the individual is trying to demonstrate mastery. The achievement behaviors will be adaptive, in that the individual will persist in the face of failure, will exert effort, select challenging tasks, and be interested in the task. On the other hand, if the individual is ego involved, then perceived ability is relevant, as the individual is trying to demonstrate normative ability, and how his or her ability fares with comparative others becomes important. If the individual is ego involved and perceives him or herself as high in ability, then that person is likely to engage in adaptive achievement behaviors. Demonstrating high normative ability in this context is likely; therefore, the individual is motivated to persist and demonstrate that competence to others. If one can demonstrate ability with little effort, however, this is evidence of even higher ability. Thus, the ego-involved person is inclined to use the least amount of effort to realize the goal of action. If the perception of ability is low, on the other hand, then the individual will realize that ability is not likely to be demonstrated, and he or she will manifest *maladaptive* achievement behaviors. Maladaptive behaviors are those in which the individual avoids challenge; reduces persistence in the face of difficulty; does not exert effort; and, in sport, drops out if achievement of desired goals appears difficult. Although the participant may view these behaviors as adaptive, because a lack of ability is disguised by these behaviors, they are maladaptive in terms of motivation and achievement.

The interesting issue is how one becomes ego- or task-involved. Two theories are generally considered. One is that individuals are predisposed to be task- or ego-oriented, which is the focus of this learning experience. The second is that the situation induces task- or ego-involvement. This is the focus of experience 18 (page 163). Individuals are assumed to be disposed toward task or ego orientation (Nicholls, 1989). Individual differences in ego or task orientation may be from socialization through task- or ego-involving situations, either in the home, the classroom, or previous physical activity experiences. The individual will exhibit the behaviors associated with each achievement goal. We must note here that the goal orientations are not to be viewed as traits. Rather, they are cognitive schema, subject to change as the individual processes information pertaining to the task performance. However, the orientations do have stability over time. One assumption of achievement goal theory is that goal orientations are orthogonal; thus, one can be high or low in either, or both, at the same time. There is now a lot of empirical evidence to support this (see Roberts, Treasure, & Kavussanu, 1997).

Much research has applied and tested the conceptual relevance of dispositional goals to the domain of sport. This research has focused on identifying the cognitive and behavioral concomitants of task and ego dispositional orientations (Duda, 1993; Roberts, 1993). It has consistently demonstrated that a conceptually coherent relationship between achievement goals and beliefs has emerged in sport. We have good means to measure the goals, and the research has demonstrated that a task goal relates to beliefs about success, an important moderator of achievement behavior. Task goals are associated with the belief that hard work and collaboration with peers lead to success. An ego goal relates to the belief that success is achieved through beating others and demonstrating superior ability. When asked about the purposes of sport, task goals are associated with enhancing self-esteem, advancing good citizenship, fostering mastery, and a physically active lifestyle, whereas ego goals are associated with enhancing one's status, career, and superiority. In terms of achievement strategies, task goals are associated with adaptive strategies, such as being committed in practice, trying hard, and persisting when difficulties or failure occur. Ego goals are associated with maladaptive strategies, such as avoiding practice, not trying hard, doing tasks they know they can do easily, and dropping out or giving up. There are relationships with affective variables, in that task-oriented people are more satisfied with their performance, enjoy practice more, and show more interest in the task. Ego-oriented athletes are less satisfied, unless they are high in ability; enjoy sport less; and display less interest.

Clearly, being task oriented is beneficial for children and youthful participants! Whether you are task or ego oriented affects your perceptions about what causes success, the purposes of sport, appropriate achievement strategies, perception of competence, and enjoyment and interest (see Roberts, Treasure, & Kavussanu, 1997).

Some interesting data relative to moral functioning has also been revealed lately. Ego-oriented athletes are more likely than task-oriented athletes to engage in cheating behavior to win games, to engage in injurious acts, and to be willing to suspend good sportspersonship in the quest to win games (Kavussanu, 1997). This is a fascinating area of future research.

Learning Experience

Purpose

To investigate the goal orientations of individuals in competitive programs and individuals in recreational programs.

Measuring Tool

Use the Perception of Success Questionnaire (POSQ) on page 112.

Procedure

1. The real task here is to select teams that are different in the degree of competition inherent in the game. Select two teams in each category, two teams in an intense competitive game versus two teams in a recreational or pickup game. Do not use a team of which you are a member. You should try to get 20 players in each category.

2. Obtain permission from the individuals in charge (if appropriate) to administer the POSQ. Administering and completing the questionnaire should take no more than 5 minutes.

3. Have each player fill out the POSQ independently, either before (preferably) or after the game. Bring enough pencils for the team members.

Analysis of Results

1. We are going to determine the task and ego orientation score for each participant. Use questions 1, 2, 3, 6, 10, and 11 to determine the score for ego orientation, and questions 4, 5, 7, 8, 9, and 12 to determine the score for task orientation. The scoring is as follows: an A is 5, a B is 4, a C is 3, a D is 2, and an E is 1. Add the score for each person and find the mean score for each person for each orientation. Use the Achievement Goal Orientation Data Table on page 113 to organize your mean scores. Total the scores for the individuals in each competitive category on both task and ego orientation.

2. If you wish, you can compare the two competitive situations by conducting a t-test on each goal orientation. However, for the purpose of the experience, comparing means visually will suffice.

Discussion Questions

1. Did the two competitive situations differ in any of the two orientations?
2. How did your results compare with previous goal orientation research in sport settings? If there were differences, can you explain them?
3. Given the goal orientations for the two populations, could you predict perceived satisfaction for the two groups?
4. How can knowledge of individual's goal orientations help teachers and coaches?

References

Atkinson, J., & Feather, N. (1966). *A theory of achievement motivation.* New York: Wiley.

Duda, J.L. (1993). A social cognitive approach to the study of motivation in sport. In R.N. Singer, M. Murphey, & L.K. Tennant (Eds.), *Handbook of research on sport psychology* (pp. 421-436). New York: Macmillan.

Kavussanu, M. (1997). *Achievement goal theory and moral functioning in sport.* Unpublished doctoral dissertation, University of Illinois, Champaign, IL.

McAuley, E., & Duncan, T.E. (1990). The causal attribution process in sport and physical activity. In S. Graham & V. Folkes (Eds.), *Advances in applied psychology V: Applications of attribution theory* (pp. 37-52). Hillsdale, NJ: Erlbaum.

Nicholls, J.G. (1989). *The competitive ethos and democratic education.* Cambridge, MA: Harvard University Press.

Roberts, G.C. (1975, October). Win-loss causal attributions of Little League players. *Seventh Symposium of Psychomotor Learning and Psychology of Sport* (pp. 315-322). Longmeadow, MA: Mouvement Publications.

Roberts, G.C. (1993). Motivation in sport: Understanding and enhancing the motivation and achievement of children. In R.N. Singer, M. Murphey, & L.K. Tennant (Eds.), *Handbook of research on sport psychology* (pp. 405-420). New York: Macmillan.

Roberts, G.C., & Pascuzzi, D. (1979). Causal attributions in sport: Some theoretical implications. *Journal of Sport Psychology, 1,* 203-211.

Roberts, G.C., Treasure, D.C., & Kavussanu, M. (1997). Motivation in physical activity contexts: An achievement goal perspective. In M. Maehr & P. Pintrich (Eds.), *Advances in motivation and achievement.* Vol. 10. (pp. 413-447). Greenwich, CT: JAI Press.

Spink, K.S. (1978). Win-loss causal attributions of high school basketball players. *Canadian Journal of Applied Sport Sciences, 3,* 195-201.

Weiner, B. (1986). *An attributional theory of motivation and emotion.* New York: Springer-Verlag.

Weiner, B., Frieze, I., Kukla, A., Reed, L., Rest, S., & Rosenhaum, R. (1971). Perceiving the causes of success and failure. In E. Jones, D. Kanouse, H. Kelley, R. Nisbett, S. Valins, & B. Weiner (Eds.), *Attribution-Perceiving the causes of behavior* (pp. 95-120). New York: Learning Press.

Perception of Success Questionnaire (Adult Version)

What does success in sport mean to you? There are no right or wrong answers. We ask you to circle the letter that best indicates how you feel.

When playing sport, I feel most successful when

	Strongly agree		Neutral		Strongly disagree
I beat other people.	A	B	C	D	E
I am clearly superior.	A	B	C	D	E
I am the best.	A	B	C	D	E
I work hard.	A	B	C	D	E
I show clear personal improvement.	A	B	C	D	E
I outperform my opponents.	A	B	C	D	E
I reach a goal.	A	B	C	D	E
I overcome difficulties.	A	B	C	D	E
I reach personal goals.	A	B	C	D	E
I win.	A	B	C	D	E
I show other people I am the best.	A	B	C	D	E
I perform to the best of my ability.	A	B	C	D	E

Achievement Goal Orientation Data Table

Competitive task	Competitive ego	Recreational task	Recreational ego
Total =	Total =	Total =	Total =
Mean =	Mean =	Mean =	Mean =

EXPERIENCE 12

INTRINSIC MOTIVATION

Why is it that some athletes are so motivated they continue to perform and enjoy performing even though they or their teams usually lose? On the other hand, some athletes are so unmotivated that coaches must continually urge them to greater effort. For professional athletes, money and recognition would seem to be enough incentive, but what about amateur athletes? What is it that keeps them participating? Answers to questions such as these are of interest to coaches and sport psychologists alike. One approach to this topic is through the body of research termed intrinsic motivation.

Objectives

In this learning experience you will learn

- the distinction between intrinsic and extrinsic motivation,
- the research paradigm for investigating intrinsic motivation questions,
- the conceptual explanations of intrinsic motivation, and
- the research findings in the area.

Then you will have the opportunity to conduct a field study in the area of intrinsic motivation and determine the level of intrinsic motivation of children involved in competitive sport.

Basic Considerations

Intrinsic motivation is defined as the motivation to engage in an activity for its own sake. Athletes who play basketball because of the enjoyment and satisfaction they get out of the sport are participating because they are intrinsically motivated. Conversely, if athletes are playing basketball to win a league trophy, they are extrinsically motivated. *Extrinsic motivation* is defined as motivation that is externally controlled.

For several years intrinsic and extrinsic motivation were considered additive, and the motivation was seen as optimal when high intrinsic motivation was combined with strong external rewards (Vroom, 1964). This may not always be the case. Several studies show that external rewards can actually *decrease* intrinsic motivation under certain conditions (Deci, 1971; Lepper & Greene, 1975; Lepper, Greene, & Nisbett, 1973).

The typical investigation of intrinsic motivation involved the following experimental procedure. Individuals were assigned to one of three conditions: *expected reward, unexpected reward,* or *no reward.* In the expected-reward condition, individuals were promised and received a reward for performing some task. In the unexpected-reward condition, the individuals received the same rewards as the reward group, even though it was not mentioned before or during the session. In the no-reward condition, the individuals neither expected nor received a reward.

Immediately following the experiment or up to several weeks later, depending on the study, participants received an opportunity to engage in the same activity. The individuals were either given no instructions or simply told to do what they wanted. The researchers took some measure of the degree to which they engaged in the same task rather than different activities. They took this measure as the operational measure of intrinsic motivation. The assumption is that, if the individual is intrinsically motivated, he or she will engage in the task. Usually, individuals in the expected-reward condition spent less time engaging in the same activity than individuals in the other two conditions. Researchers have posited several theoretical positions to explain this finding.

One explanation for the decreased time spent on the same activity by the individuals in the expected-reward condition is referred to as the *overjustification hypothesis* (Lepper, Greene, & Nisbett, 1973). This hypothesis states that an individual's intrinsic interest in an activity may be decreased by inducing him or her to engage in that activity as a means to some extrinsic reward. In other words, if the external reward is psychologically oversufficient, the individual infers that his behavior was motivated by external rewards rather than by intrinsic interest in the activity.

A second explanation is based on *cognitive-evaluation theory* (Deci, 1975). Deci argues that individuals want to be self-determining and in control of their lives. Accordingly, individuals evaluate the meaning of rewards. If the interpretation of the reward suggests that it is given to control behavior (e.g., a parent stating that if a child continues to play the piano, he or she will receive ice cream later), then the reward undermines level of interest in the task. The reward is interpreted as controlling behavior and interest wanes. Playing is attributed to the reward, not to interest in the task. If the reward is interpreted as providing information relevant to one's own competence at the task, however, the reward may enhance motivation if interpretations of information suggest competence. Of course, if the reward provides information suggesting low competence, it may undermine interest. The controlling or information aspect of the reward is important to consider.

In summary, several theoretical approaches predict similar outcomes yet differ in their explanations of why the phenomenon occurs. At present none of the theories has full support, but the attributional approach reflected in the overjustification hypothesis and cognitive-evaluation explanations seems to enjoy the most recognition. In sport, the cognitive-evaluation explanation is the most used (cf. Vallerand & Reid, 1984).

This research questions the desirability of giving rewards for success and participation in athletics. Apparently, if a reward is promised and expected, it lessens interest and motivation in the activity. Some research has even shown that an unexpected reward causes children to attribute the reason for their participation to the reward and to be subsequently less motivated (Kruglanski, Alan, & Lewis, 1972). Thus, using rewards as motivators for athletic success and participation may be detrimental (Stratton & Pierce, 1981; Weinberg, 1981, 1984).

Sports at all levels have traditionally included rewards in the form of trophies, ribbons, medals, and the like. Available research suggests that giving rewards has the opposite effect of the one desired. This effect appears to be most salient when noncontingent rewards are used, that is, rewards based only on participation and not contingent on the individual's performance. Several studies have found that noncontingent rewards tend to have a larger undermining-of-interest effect (Orlick & Mosher, 1978; Thomas & Tennant, 1978).

What are the implications of this research for physical education and athletics? In one line of reasoning, using Deci's (1975) arguments, Ryan (1977) suggested that college athletes on athletic grants or scholarships may view themselves as performing for money and, thus, display less intrinsic motivation than athletes not on scholarship. Supportive of his suggestion, Ryan found that football players on scholarship exhibited less intrinsic motivation than nonscholarship football players.

Interestingly, Ryan (1977) predicted the obverse for females. Ryan's explanation for this apparent paradox emanates from Deci's work on the informational and controlling properties associated with rewards. Informational rewards should increase intrinsic motivation, whereas rewards viewed as controlling should decrease intrinsic motivation. Ryan postulates that males on athletic scholarships view the scholarship as controlling and, as a result, exhibit decreased intrinsic motivation. Females, on the other hand, view the athletic scholarship as positive information concerning their competence, because of the novelty of athletic scholarships for women. Women, therefore, should show a concomitant increase in intrinsic motivation.

Ryan (1980) confirmed this speculation in a subsequent study. He found that female athletes on scholarship enjoyed their sport significantly more than their nonscholarship counterparts. Interestingly, he found the results for males differed by sport. For football players, the results replicated his previous studies. For wrestlers, the results revealed the opposite effect—those wrestlers on scholarship were more motivated in their sport than nonscholarship wrestlers. Ryan (1980) speculated that, because few wrestlers get scholarships, those who do so must be good, and as a result they make competence attributions.

The results of these studies reveal that giving rewards, whether money or trophies and so forth, may cause a decline in the intrinsic motivation of athletes, particularly children. Recently, the area of intrinsic motivation in physical activity has received a boost from the excellent work of Vallerand and his colleagues (e.g., Vallerand & Reid, 1990; Pelletier et al., 1995). As part of his work into the motivational equation, Vallerand now argues that intrinsic motivation includes three categories. First is the *intrinsic motivation to know*, in that some people perform an activity for the pleasure and satisfaction they experience in learning, exploring, or trying to understand something. The second type is an *intrinsic motivation toward accomplishment*, in which an individual wants to demonstrate mastery or create something. The third type is an *intrinsic motivation to experience stimulation*, in which someone engages in sport to experience excitement and other stimulating sensations. Thus, a new and exciting era in understanding motivation in sport is opening, with researchers such as Vallerand trying to determine the components of what makes each of us motivated to participate in sport. Vallerand's crucial message is that intrinsic motivation is a global construct and, to understand it, we need to know and consider the different types of intrinsic motivations. Clearly, we need more research in this important area.

The learning experience will allow you to obtain a better understanding of the degree of intrinsic or extrinsic motivation reported by children engaged in formal or informal sport settings.

Learning Experience

Purpose

To investigate the intrinsic motivation of children who are engaged in either an organized sport program (leading to a league championship) or an informal sport program.

Measuring Tools

Intrinsic Motivation Questionnaire on page 121 and Intrinsic Motivation Data Sheet on page 122.

Procedure

1. Select 10 children who compete in an organized sport experience, that is, a competitive league structured and administered by adults that culminates in a league championship. Be certain that the children are at least 11 or 12 years of age. Select 10 children who participate only in informal sport, that is, any spontaneous athletic activity initiated and administered by the children themselves. A pickup game of basketball children organized in the local park would be a suitable sample. Again, be certain the children are at least 11 or 12 years of age.

2. Be sure that the subjects in the informal condition do *not* participate in any organized sport.

3. Hand out the Intrinsic Motivation Questionnaire and a pencil to each child.

4. Have each child respond to the question and emphasize that he or she should be careful to put down the most important reason.

Analysis of Results

Because each child gives his or her own response, you must analyze each response by using content-analysis procedures (see page 25). Determine whether the subjects' responses conform to one of the following categories. These categories, included here to help you with your analysis, have been taken from Maehr (1984) and Roberts (1984). They have suggested broad motivational goal categories that you can designate when considering motivation patterns. These categories may be subsumed within the two broader categories of intrinsic and extrinsic motivation. For the purpose of this experience, if the subject gives more than one reason, score the first response only.

Intrinsic Goals

Task or sport mastery goal.

- Responses that refer to mastering a skill, feeling competent, doing well in sport, having fun, and enjoying the task or sport.
- The child seems to participate in the game or task for its own sake and enjoys participation.

Ego or competition goal.

- All responses related to doing better than some socially defined standard, usually peers.
- Responses that involve beating someone, doing better than someone else, winning, or being the best fall within this category.

Extrinsic Goals

Social approval goal.

- Score responses that involve pleasing significant others or making others happy as social approval goals. Pleasing the coach, pleasing friends or teammates, making parents happy fall within this category.

Extrinsic rewards.

- Score all comments such as "participate for the rewards" or "the trophies" or "the trips" within this category.

1. Record the results on the Intrinsic Motivation Data Sheet.
2. Total the responses in each category.
3. Total the responses in the internal and external categories.

Discussion Questions

1. What are the differences in the internal and external response categories for each group?

2. We would expect individuals in the organized sport group to be more externally oriented. Is that what happened? If not, why not?

3. Within each category, it is likely the informal group would score higher on task and the organized sport group would score higher on social approval. Is that what happened? Why or why not?

4. If other members of your class had a sample from the opposite sex, compare your results and see if any sex differences occur. Are there any? Can you think of why girls might be different from boys?

5. What implications do your findings have for organized sport? Would you change the structure of organized sport in some way to enhance intrinsic motivation?

References

Deci, E. (1971). Effects of externally mediated rewards on intrinsic motivation. *Journal of Personality and Social Psychology, 18,* 105-115.

Deci, E. (1975). *Intrinsic motivation.* New York: Plenum Press.

Kruglanski, A., Alan, S., & Lewis, T. (1972). Retrospective misattribution and task enjoyment. *Journal of Experimental Social Psychology, 8,* 493-501.

Lepper, M., & Greene, D. (1975). Turning play into work: Effects of adult surveillance and extrinsic rewards on children's intrinsic motivation. *Journal of Personality and Social Psychology, 31,* 479-486.

Lepper, M., Greene, D., & Nisbett, R. (1973). Undermining children's intrinsic interest with extrinsic rewards. *Journal of Personality and Social Psychology, 28,* 129-137.

Maehr, M L. (1984). Meaning and motivation: Toward a theory of personal investment. In R. Ames & C. Ames (Eds.), *Research in motivation in education: Student motivation* (pp. 115-144). New York: Academic Press.

Orlick, T.D., & Mosher, R. (1978). Extrinsic awards and participant motivation in a sport related task. *International Journal of Sport Psychology, 9,* 27-39.

Pelletier, L.G., Fortier, M.S., Vallerand, R.J., Tuson, K.M., Briere, N.M., & Blais, M.R. (1995). Toward a new measure of intrinsic motivation, extrinsic motivation, and amotivation in sports: The sport motivation scale (SMS). *Journal of Sport & Exercise Psychology, 17,* 35-53.

Roberts, G.C. (1984). Toward a new theory of sport motivation: The role of perceived ability. In J. Silva & R. Weinberg (Eds.), *Psychological foundations of sport and exercise* (pp. 214-228). Champaign, IL: Human Kinetics.

Ryan, E. (1977). *Attribution, intrinsic motivation, and athletics.* Paper presented at the annual meeting of the National College Physical Education Association for Men, Orlando, Florida.

Ryan, E. (1980). Attribution, intrinsic motivation and athletics: A replication and extension. In C.H. Nadeau, W.R. Halliwell, K.M. Newell, & G.C. Roberts (Eds.), *Psychology of motor behavior and sport—1979* (pp. 19-26). Champaign, IL: Human Kinetics.

Stratton, R.R., & Pierce, W.J. (1981). Motivation and rewards in youth sports. *Journal of Sport Behavior, 3,* 147-157.

Thomas, J.R., & Tennant, L.K. (1978). Effects of rewards on changes in children's motivation for an athletic task. In F. Smoll & R. Smith (Eds.), *Psychological perspectives in youth sports* (pp.123-144). Washington, DC: Hemisphere.

Vallerand, R.J., & Reid, G. (1984). On the causal effects of perceived competence on intrinsic motivation: A test of the cognitive evaluation theory. *Journal of Sport Psychology, 6,* 94-102.

Vallerand, R.J., & Reid, G. (1990). Motivation and special populations: Theory, research, and implications regarding motor behavior. In G. Reid (Ed.), *Problems in movement control* (pp. 159-197). New York: North Holland.

Vroom, V. (1964). *Motivation and work.* New York: Wiley.

Weinberg, R.S. (1981). Why kids play or do not play organized sports. *The Physical Educator, 38,* 71-76.

Weinberg, R.S. (1984). The relationship between extrinsic rewards and intrinsic motivation in sport. In J.M. Silva & R.W. Weinberg (Eds.), *Psychological foundations of sport* (pp.177-187). Champaign, IL: Human Kinetics.

Intrinsic Motivation Questionnaire

Why do you participate in sport activities such as the one you are playing here? Think carefully, and write down your most important reason.

Intrinsic Motivation Data Sheet

	Organized sport				Informal sport			
	Internal goals		External goals		Internal goals		External goals	
Subject	Task	Ego	Social approval	Extrinsic	Task	Ego	Social approval	Extrinsic
1								
2								
3								
4								
5								
6								
7								
8								
9								
10								
Totals								

EXPERIENCE 13

COHESION

There is no doubt that cohesion is an important concept for both practitioners and those within the research community. From the practitioners' viewpoint, we often hear that a champion team will beat a team of champions. The importance of this for practitioners parallels the research perspective, as cohesion is a frequently studied group concept in sport science (Widmeyer, Brawley, & Carron, 1992).

Objectives

In this learning experience you will learn

- the definition of cohesion,
- a conceptual model of cohesion, and
- the important antecedents and consequences of cohesion.

Then you will have the opportunity to determine whether the degree of cohesion influences psychological momentum and predicted game outcome.

Basic Considerations

Given the importance of cohesion within both the applied and research areas, we would surmise that we would understand what the term means. Until recently, however, this has not been the case. Cohesion has been defined in many ways throughout the years. In recent times, Carron (1982) has defined cohesiveness as a "dynamic process which is reflected in the tendency for a group to stick together and remain united in the pursuit of its goals and objectives" (p. 124). It is this definition that has generated the most interest in the recent cohesion literature.

Although the definition of cohesion has evolved over time, the most important evolution may involve its movement from a unidimensional to a multidimensional concept. For many years, cohesion was viewed as a unidimensional concept that we could assess using a singular measurement. Although the measurement changed (i.e., interpersonal attraction, versus attraction to the group, versus commitment to the group, etc.), the fact remained that cohesion was still seen as a unidimensional concept. However, in the last decade a call was made within sport to consider cohesion as a multidimensional construct (Carron, Widmeyer, & Brawley, 1985).

In the sporting context, Carron et al. (1985) developed a conceptual model, which they then used to develop an instrument to measure cohesiveness. The conceptual model portrays cohesion as a multidimensional construct that includes task and social cohesion, each of which reflects an individual (e.g., beliefs each member holds about personal benefits of their group membership) and group (e.g., beliefs members hold about the total group) orientation. This results in four manifestations of cohesion in sport groups: individual attractions to the group—task; individual attractions to the group—social; group integration—task; and group integration—social. These four related facets act together in creating an integrated perception of cohesion.

It was from this conceptual model that Carron et al. (1985) developed the Group Environment Questionnaire (GEQ) to assess the cohesiveness of sport teams. The GEQ, which assesses the four facets of cohesion we have outlined, is the instrument that is currently used most to assess cohesion in activity-based settings.

With cohesion now defined in a meaningful way, we can turn our attention to what the research says about the antecedents and consequences of cohesion. Carron (1982) proposed a framework that incorporates antecedents and consequences of cohesiveness. There are four proposed antecedents of cohesion—environmental factors, leadership factors, personal factors, and team factors—and two proposed consequences—individual and group factors. We will now present selected studies to illustrate each category.

As mentioned, there are two categories of consequences—group and individual outcomes. Without doubt, most research on the consequences of cohesiveness has examined group outcomes, with team success the variable of choice. Given the homage that coaches and athletes pay to the proposed association between cohesion and team success, the scientific results are surprising, in that the results supporting the relationship are mixed. However, Carron (1988) has noted that there are more studies demonstrating a positive relationship between these two variables and that most studies suggesting a negative relationship were done with coacting teams, in which cohesion is not as important to team success.

For individual outcomes, two variables that have been investigated include individual satisfaction and individual adherence. The results of research have shown that individual satisfaction with the physical activity experience (Carron & Spink, 1993) is greater when group cohesiveness is perceived as high. Similar findings have been found for individual adherence behavior. In the exercise setting, it has been found that individual adherence to exercise programs was associated with increased levels of group cohesion (Spink & Carron, 1994).

Knowing that cohesion has important consequences for the individual and the group, the question becomes: What are the factors that might cause cohesion? Regarding environmental determinants as antecedents, one factor that has received attention is group size. Researchers and theoreticians have had an enduring interest in the influence of size on group dynamics. They have observed that increasing group size has numerous effects for individual members. In a series of studies in the exercise setting, Carron and Spink (1995, Studies 1 & 2) found that participants in smaller exercise groups held significantly greater perceptions of their group's task and social cohesiveness than did participants in larger groups.

Although personal determinants can play an important role in the amount of cohesiveness that develops in a group, little research has been conducted to date. One research area that looks promising, however, concerns the relationship between the personality trait of self-handicapping and perceptions of group cohesion. Self-handicapping represents the strategies individuals use to protect their self-esteem with excuses for forthcoming events. Carron, Prapavessis, and Grove (1994) examined the relationship between self-handicapping and cohesiveness in a sample of male athletes. Their results revealed a negative relationship between the trait of self-handicapping and perceptions of the group's cohesiveness. If this can be replicated, it suggests that the development of cohesiveness within a group may be more difficult if the individuals within the group are all high self-handicappers.

A third proposed category of antecedents, as identified by Carron (1982), is leadership determinants. In the sport setting, we might expect that developing cohesiveness would be associated with the behavior of the coach. Research conducted in the sport setting has provided support for this supposition. Specifically, it has been found with ringette teams (Spink, 1998) that specific types of leadership behavior (e.g., training and instruction) are associated with increased levels of perceived social cohesiveness within the team.

There also have been some attempts to provide leaders in sport and exercise with techniques they could use to enhance cohesiveness within their groups through team-building interventions. In the exercise realm, Carron and Spink (1993) assessed the effects of a team-building intervention, which they introduced to exercise leaders to implement, on the development of cohesiveness within exercise classes. The results revealed that participants in the team-building groups expressed greater task cohesiveness than did participants in control classes.

To further test the effects of team building on cohesiveness, Carron and Spink (1995, Study 4) examined how a team-building protocol would influence perceptions of cohesion in small and large exercise groups. Although previous research in the exercise setting has revealed an inverse relationship between size of the group and cohesiveness (Carron & Spink, 1995, Studies 1 & 2), the results of Carron and Spink (1995, Study 4) revealed that a team-building intervention offset the negative impact increased size can have on perceptions of cohesiveness. Specifically, no differences in perceptions of cohesiveness were found for participants in small (less than 20 participants) or large (more than 40 participants) exercise classes when they had been exposed to a team-building intervention.

The last category of potential antecedents is team determinants. The idea behind this category is that shared group experiences may impact the development of cohesiveness. One example of a possible team determinant of cohesiveness is group goal setting for a team. In a study examining this relationship, Brawley, Carron, and Widmeyer (1993) explored how the amount of perceived participative goal setting related to perceptions of group cohesiveness. The results from their study revealed that participation in goal setting was strongly related to perceptions of group cohesiveness in athletes.

As this discussion reveals, cohesion is a complex concept that incorporates several antecedents and consequences. Further, we hope it is now clear that the importance of understanding cohesion goes beyond looking at its relationship with team success. In fact, other researchers (cf. Widmeyer et al., 1992) have suggested that there are many other antecedents and consequences of cohesion that deserve the attention of future research. Clearly, we need more research to fully investigate the relationship between cohesion and these important antecedents and consequences. In the learning experience, you will get the opportunity to investigate the relationship between cohesiveness and a new consequence—psychological momentum. Recent research has found that perceptions of psychological momentum are greatest when perceptions of task cohesion are high (Eisler & Spink, 1998).

Learning Experience

Purpose

To investigate the relationship between perceptions of cohesiveness, psychological momentum, and predicted performance outcomes.

Measuring Tools

Cohesion Questionnaire on page 128 (adapted from Eisler & Spink, 1998) and Cohesion Data Sheet on page 130.

Procedure

1. Split the class into two equal groups. Ensure that there are an equal number of males and females in each group.

2. Have the members of the first group independently read and answer the questions in Situation A and those in the second group read and answer the questions in Situation B.

Analysis of Results

1. Enter the score of each question in the Cohesion Data Sheet.

2. For psychological momentum, is there a significant difference between highly cohesive (Situation A) and less cohesive (Situation B) teams? For this analysis, you will need to conduct a t-test (see page 38).

3. For game expectancy, is there a significant difference between highly cohesive (Situation A) and less cohesive (Situation B) teams? For this analysis, you also will need to conduct a t test (see page 38).

Discussion Questions

1. Do your scores support the hypothesis that psychological momentum is higher for cohesive teams?

2. Do your scores support the hypothesis that predictions for game outcome are higher for cohesive teams?

3. What do your results indicate for psychological momentum and game predictions for less cohesive teams?

4. Do your results provide any practical information for coaches and athletes?

References

Brawley, L.R., Carron, A.V., & Widmeyer, W.N. (1993). The influence of the group and its cohesiveness on perceptions of group goal-related variables. *Journal of Sport & Exercise Psychology, 15,* 245-260.

Carron, A.V. (1982). Cohesiveness in sport groups: Interpretations and considerations. *Journal of Sport Psychology, 4,* 123-138.

Carron, A.V. (1988). *Group dynamics in sport.* London, ON: Spodym.

Carron, A.V., Prapavessis, H., & Grove, J.R. (1994). Group effects and self-handicapping. *Journal of Sport & Exercise Psychology, 16,* 246-257.

Carron, A.V., & Spink, K.S. (1993). Team building in an exercise setting. *The Sport Psychologist, 7*, 8-18.

Carron, A.V., & Spink, K.S. (1995). The group size-cohesion relationship in exercise groups. *Small Group Research, 26*, 86-105.

Carron, A.V., Widmeyer, W.N., & Brawley, L.R. (1985). The development of an instrument to assess cohesion in sport teams: The Group Environment Questionnaire. *Journal of Sport Psychology, 7*, 244-266.

Eisler, L., & Spink, K.S. (1998). Effects of scoring configuration and task cohesion on the perception of psychological momentum. *Journal of Sport & Exercise Psychology, 20*, 310-319.

Spink, K.S. (1998). Mediational effects of social cohesion on the leadership behavior—intention to return relationship in sport. *Group dynamics: theory, research, and practice, 2*, 92-100.

Spink, K.S., & Carron, A.V. (1994). Group cohesion effects in exercise classes. *Small Group Research, 25*, 26-42.

Widmeyer, W.N., Brawley, L.R., & Carron, A.V. (1992). Group dynamics in sport. In T.S. Horn (Ed.), *Advances in sport psychology* (pp. 163-180). Champaign, IL: Human Kinetics.

Cohesion Questionnaire

Situation A

Coaches and athletes often talk about factors associated with winning and losing in team sports. One factor that emerges frequently is team cohesion.

Imagine that you are playing on a volleyball team that is very cohesive. That is, during the present season, your team has gone through numerous situations including successes and failures, which have drawn the team members together. The coaching staff has actively encouraged the development of cohesion through opportunities to create team goals and for the players to get to know one another on a personal level. All the players on the team are close and are united in pursuing the goals of the team as a whole. The players understand and accept their individual roles on the team and feel they are contributing to and responsible for the team successes.

Imagine your team is playing a best-of-three match (15-point game) against an opponent who is evenly matched with you. Your team has played this opponent on four occasions, and each team has won twice, alternating wins.

The following describes a hypothetical situation in a *fifth* meeting between your team and this opponent. Please read the situation and answer the two questions that follow. There are no right or wrong answers. Circle the number you think best answers the question.

Game Situation

In the third game of a best-of-three game match, your opponents were leading your team 13-8. However, your team came back to tie the score 13-13 quickly, using only two servers to score the 5 points. Your team has the serve. Remember, you are playing on a cohesive team, one in which there is a strong tendency for members to stick together while remaining united in pursuing the team's goals and objectives.

1. Which team has the momentum?

1 2 3 4 5 6 7 8 9 10 11
Definitely your team   **Definitely the opposition**

2. Which team will win this game?

1 2 3 4 5 6 7 8 9 10 11
Definitely your team   **Definitely the opposition**

Situation B

Coaches and athletes often talk about factors that are associated with winning and losing in team sports. One factor that emerges quite frequently is team cohesion.

Imagine that you are playing on a volleyball team that is not cohesive. The coaching staff has not actively encouraged the development of cohesion during the season. The members of the team do not share common team goals and the players have not had the opportunity to get to know one another on a personal level. Some players feel that their role on the team is unimportant, and others are unclear of their individual role and responsibility within the team. Most members do not value the experiences and time they spend with this team.

Imagine your team is playing a best-of-three match (15-point game) against an opponent who is evenly matched with you. Your team has played this opponent on four occasions, and each team has won twice, alternating wins.

The following describes a hypothetical situation in a *fifth* meeting between your team and this opponent. Please read the situation and answer the two questions that follow. There are no right or wrong answers. Circle the number you think best answers the question.

Game Situation

In the third game of a best-of-three game match, your opponents were leading your team 13-8. However, your team came back to tie the score 13-13 quickly, using only two servers to score the 5 points. Your team has the serve. Remember, you are playing on a team that lacks cohesiveness, one in which there is little tendency for members to stick together or remain united in pursuing the team's goals and objectives.

1. Which team has the momentum?

1 2 3 4 5 6 7 8 9 10 11
Definitely your team   **Definitely the opposition**

2. Which team will win this game?

1 2 3 4 5 6 7 8 9 10 11
Definitely your team   **Definitely the opposition**

Cohesion Data Sheet

Individual	Situation A		Situation B	
	Psychological Momentum	Game Prediction	Psychological Momentum	Game Prediction
1				
2				
3				
4				
5				
6				
7				
8				
9				
10				
Totals				

Note: A lower score reflects greater psychological momentum and greater game prediction.

PART III

APPLYING SPORT PSYCHOLOGICAL PHENOMENA

EXPERIENCE 14

PHYSICAL RELAXATION

To say that muscular contraction is an important part of performing in sport might be the classic understatement. To move around a tennis court, throw a football, shoot a puck, or sprint down a track effectively require specific degrees of muscular contraction. Unfortunately, in sport we sometimes use too much muscular contraction, the result being a less than stellar performance. These unwanted muscular contractions are often the by-products of experiencing stress in the competitive setting. As mentioned in the Anxiety Learning Experience (chapter 9), muscle tension is often a by-product of the stress response. In many cases, athletes are not even aware that they are tense. However, the signs are there, if you look for them. Some warning signs that the muscles are excessively tight include butterflies in the stomach, tenseness around the shoulders, or legs that feel like cement blocks. Although these are entirely normal reactions to competitive stress and are experienced by most athletes, excessive amounts will hamper physical performance. For this reason, teaching athletes how to physically relax is an important element in preventing excessive muscular tension and, thus, a key to improving sport performance.

Objectives

In this learning experience, you will learn

- why it is important to be able to relax in a sport situation,
- the steps to follow to develop relaxation skill, and
- how to develop a cassette tape as a guide for relaxation sessions.

Then you will have the opportunity to learn a relaxation technique that you can use effectively to reduce muscle tension.

Basic Considerations

The investigation of peak performance in sport over the years has revealed that physical relaxation is a condition often associated with great performances (Garfield & Bennett, 1984). In a study of top amateur and professional golfers, for example, Cohn (1991) found that feeling physically relaxed was a condition cited as being associated with peak performance. Conversely, it has been documented in recent research that the poorest performances of athletes are associated with elevated levels of somatic anxiety (Burton, 1988). We can manifest somatic anxiety, which refers to the physiological and affective elements that develop directly from autonomic arousal, in many ways—elevated heart rate, sweaty palms, and butterflies in the stomach (Martens, Vealey, & Burton, 1990). Another manifestation is increased tension within the muscle. This increase in muscle tension may interrupt the coordination of motor skills that, in turn, affect performance (Weinberg & Hunt, 1976).

The preceding results suggest that practicing some form of muscle relaxation may prove beneficial in maximizing performance by keeping tension manageable. As noted by Harris and Williams (1993), learning muscle relaxation also has other uses. These include removing localized tension (e.g., the muscle tension that might result from an injury), facilitating recovery when fatigued, and helping the onset of sleep the night before competition.

Although there are several muscle relaxation techniques currently available, the one in this Learning Experience was developed by Edmund Jacobson (1938). A physician by trade, Jacobson observed that patients who were stressed often exhibited high levels of muscular tension in the face, neck, and back regions. Further, those with the highest levels of muscle tension seemed to take the most time to recover. Jacobson reasoned that he could expedite recovery in these patients by helping them reduce this muscle tension. Unfortunately, simply making the patients more aware of their tension and asking them to relax did not work. Jacobson realized that the patients would need more help in relaxing their muscles. To this end, he developed an isometric contraction-relaxation cycle to help individual patients identify the differences between tension and relaxation in muscles. This contrast between a total isometric contraction and complete muscle relaxation served as an aid to learning the difference between relaxed muscle sensation and those sensations at high muscle tension. The comparison allowed the individual to detect muscle tension when it occurred anywhere in the body. Using this technique patients were able to effectively reduce tension in their skeletal muscles on demand.

In Jacobson's relaxation technique, the individual systematically contracts then relaxes each major muscle group in the body, while focusing on the sensations felt in the muscle. Relaxation training sessions require an environment with few distractions. A carpeted, darkened room with little noise interruption would be ideal. The individual begins the session by lying on his or her back and performing an isometric contraction of a major muscle group. The contraction is held for approximately 5 to 7 seconds. After the isometric contraction, the individual relaxes the muscle as much as possible and concentrates on the feelings as the muscle relaxes. This process is repeated for each major muscle group in the body. A more complete explanation of progressive relaxation training is available in Bernstein and Borkovec (1973).

This technique usually takes 15 to 20 minutes to complete initially, but you can decrease the time to achieve total body relaxation with practice so that total body relaxation can become almost automatic. As it becomes easier to detect muscle tension and reduce the tension level, the individual can learn to relax the entire body without going through the isometric contraction-relaxation cycle for each muscle group. He or she can use these procedures to reduce muscle tension that will contribute to the control of arousal levels during competitive sport contests. Also, there is evidence to indicate that athletes using a muscle relaxation technique can reduce significantly the amount of somatic anxiety they experience before a competitive event (Maynard & Cotton, 1993). Many athletes acquire control through using a trigger perception. For some athletes, the color light blue serves as the trigger, but any trigger relevant to the athletes will work.

Although Jacobson's relaxation technique is not a panacea for any perceived overarousal level, it can help produce relaxation when the demands of the competitive situation are so high that arousal can damage performance. The learning experience will give you the opportunity to learn the technique.

Learning Experience

Purpose

To investigate the relationship between arousal and physical relaxation.

Measuring Tool

Relaxation Log on page 138.

Procedure

In this learning experience you will make a tape recording of instructions that lead you through Jacobson's progressive relaxation technique. After making the tape, use it as a personal guide during sessions when you practice the technique. You also will record heart rate data to determine the effects of the technique on arousal levels.

1. Use the following script to make your tape recording. Before recording, practice reading the script aloud several times, using a soft tone of voice that will not be distracting when you are relaxing.

"Lie down on your back." (pause)

"Place your arms comfortably at your sides and your feet uncrossed in a comfortable position." (pause)

"Slow your breathing down. Count '1' as you inhale and '2' as you exhale." (pause)

"Now, focus on the muscles in your forehead." (pause)

"Make a frown and contract those muscles. Hold the frown." (pause 5 seconds)

"Now, let go and totally relax your forehead muscles. Feel the tension flow out. You should feel no tension in your forehead." (pause)

"Focus on the muscles in your face." (pause)

"Now, contract all those muscles in your face, bite down, and squint your eyes. Feel the tension in your face." (pause)

"Let go all at once and relax your face. Feel all of the tension flow out." (pause)

"Mentally scan to see if there is any tension in your face or forehead." (pause)

"If you feel tension anywhere, contract that muscle." (pause)

"Focus on your neck and the muscles in your neck." (pause)

"Contract those muscles hard." (pause)

"Relax! Feel the tightness and tension flow out." (pause)

"Now, make a fist with your right hand and tighten your arm muscles. Hold the contraction tightly." (pause)

"Relax. Relax your hand and arm. Feel the muscles relax and the tension flow out." (pause) (Repeat, substituting the left hand and arm.)

"Your upper body should feel warm and relaxed. If you feel any muscle tension, go back and tighten and relax those muscles." (pause)

"Now, tighten your hip muscles as hard as you can and hold the contraction." (pause)

"Relax those muscles all at once and feel the tension flow out." (pause)

"Mentally scan your body to see if you feel any tightness." (pause)

"Contract the thigh muscles in your right leg and hold the muscles tightly." (pause)

"Relax. Relax your thigh and feel the muscle relax." (pause)

(Repeat for the left leg.)

"Now, point your right toe and contract your calf muscle. Hold the contraction tightly." (pause)

"Let go all at once and feel the muscle relax, the tightness flow out." (pause)

(Repeat for the left calf.)

"If you feel any tightness or tension anywhere in your body go back and contract and relax that muscle group." (pause)

"Your body should feel warm and relaxed, and it should feel heavy and totally relaxed. Focus on this relaxed feeling." (pause)

"Slowly open your eyes. You are now ready to take your heart rate."

2. When you finish making your tape, begin the next step in the learning experience. Please read all the directions before you listen to the tape. For this experience you will need a watch; your daily Relaxation Log; a pencil; your tape and tape recorder; and quiet, darkened surroundings.

3. Before you begin the relaxation session, take your heart rate, counting beats for 10 seconds then multiplying by 6 to determine the rate per minute. Record this number in your log chart as the presession heart rate.

4. After listening to your tape and completing the relaxation session, but before you get up, take your heart rate again and record it in the Relaxation Log as the postsession heart rate. Take a few minutes to move your arms and legs so that when you stand up you will not feel light-headed from lack of blood to the brain.

5. Repeat the relaxation session every day for a week, recording your heart rate before and after each session. As the week progresses, you may not need to go through each major muscle group with the contraction-relaxation cycle. You may need to focus only on the specific muscle groups that you have difficulty relaxing.

Analysis of Results

Use a t-test to determine if a difference exists between presession heart rates and postsession heart rates (see page 38).

Discussion Questions

1. Did your heart rate change from the presession to the postsession?
2. How did you respond to the sessions as you had more practice?
3. Was there any muscle group you had difficulty getting relaxed or keeping relaxed?

References

Bernstein, D.A., & Borkovec, T.D. (1973). *Progressive relaxation training: A manual for therapists.* Champaign, IL: Research Press.

Burton, D. (1988). Do anxious swimmers swim slower?: Reexamining the elusive anxiety-performance relationship. *Journal of Sport & Exercise Psychology, 10,* 45-61.

Cohn, P.J. (1991). An exploratory study on peak performance in golf. *The Sport Psychologist, 5,* 1-14.

Garfield, C.A., & Bennett, M.Z. (1984). *Peak performance: Mental training techniques of the world's greatest athletes.* Los Angeles: Tarcher.

Harris, D.V., & Williams, J.M. (1993). Relaxation and energizing techniques for regulation of arousal. In J.M. Williams (Ed.), *Applied sport psychology: Personal growth to peak performance* (2nd ed., pp. 185-199). Mountainview, CA: Mayfield.

Jacobson, E. (1938). *Progressive relaxation.* Chicago: University of Chicago Press.

Martens, R., Vealey, R.S., & Burton, D. (1990). *Competitive anxiety in sport.* Champaign, IL: Human Kinetics.

Maynard, I.W., & Cotton, P.C.J. (1993). An investigation of two stress-management techniques in a field setting. *The Sport Psychologist, 7,* 375-387.

Weinberg, R.S., & Hunt, V.U. (1976). The interrelationships between anxiety, motor performance and electromyography. *Journal of Motor Behavior, 9,* 219-224.

Relaxation Log

	Presession heart rate (beats/min)	Postsession heart rate (beats/min)
Day 1	_____	_____
Day 2	_____	_____
Day 3	_____	_____
Day 4	_____	_____
Day 5	_____	_____
Day 6	_____	_____
Day 7	_____	_____

EXPERIENCE 15

MOTOR IMAGERY

In simple terms, imagery is the process whereby an individual sees and feels pictures or images in the mind. It also is a tool that elite athletes have been using for years to maximize their competitive performance. Jean-Claude Killy, one of only two individuals to win three gold medals in alpine skiing in the same Olympics, reported that he always mentally went through each gate on the ski course as he stood in the starting gate. Similarly, the great professional golfer Jack Nicklaus reported that he never hit a golf ball until he visually saw himself hitting the ball in his mind. In fact, there would be few athletes competing at elite levels anywhere who would not use imagery systematically in practice and competition.

Objectives

In this learning experience, you will learn

- how sport competitors are using motor imagery,
- the steps involved in practicing motor imagery,
- the sensory dimensions involved in imagery, and
- imagery exercises to improve vividness and controllability in the sensory dimensions.

Then you will have the opportunity to assess your present motor-imagery skill and practice imagery to enhance your skill level.

Basic Considerations

The systematic study of imagery and its relationship to sport performance is not a new research topic. Motor imagery research began in the early 1900s with Jacobson (1930) reporting minute muscle firings, recorded by EMG (electromyogram) activity patterns, that occurred as a subject imaged limb movement. This led researchers to suggest that images caused the transmission of impulses to the muscles involved in the skill being imaged. This was assumed to help the athlete rehearse the activity or skill and warm up the mind and body in preparation for the activity.

There have been several other explanations advanced over the years about why imagery works. The currently accepted explanation suggests that imagery helps an individual develop a mental blueprint of the action required by creating a motor program in the nervous system (Murphy & Jowdy, 1992). This stored blueprint then serves as a guide for future skill reproduction.

Although using imagery is often associated with learning new sport skills, athletes use imagery for several different purposes (Orlick & Partington, 1988). Some other uses include building confidence, helping to correct a skill, preparing to get the most out of a practice or specific drill, assisting with psychological recovery (e.g., coping), and motivation (e.g., seeing yourself standing on the podium with the gold medal hanging around your neck).

In terms of the relationship between imagery and performance, the evidence suggesting that motor imagery can result in improved sport performance is equivocal (Murphy & Jowdy, 1992). One reason may be the insufficient imagery training that the subjects in these studies experience. Individuals must have sufficient training in imagery to be able to use the technique properly. Telling an individual to imagine doing the task is one thing, but does he or she do it? Just as individuals vary in levels of physical skill, they can also vary in their levels of skill at producing vivid and controlled images.

To be a proficient imager, you need to consider the following factors.

For an image to be effective, it must be vivid (Ryan & Simons, 1982). The vividness of an image relates to the degree that all senses are involved. A softball player imaging the slide into home plate should be able to see, feel, sense the emotion, and hear the sounds associated with the actual sliding action into the plate. Vividness also is associated with the clarity of the image. Are the sight, feel, emotion, and sound of the sliding action clear, or are they fuzzy? A point worth considering about vividness is that there appear to be individual differences in the ability to get vivid images using all the senses. For example, some athletes may have difficulty getting a clear visual image, but have no difficulty sensing the feel of a movement.

Another key ingredient in an effective image is the idea of controllability (Richardson, 1967). Athletes need to control their images to facilitate the required blueprinting of the correct movement pattern. Controllability refers to how well the individual can manipulate or alter the image according to his or her wishes. In other words, can you make the image do what you want it to do? Although this might seem like an easy task, there are many athletes who have difficulty controlling images. Athletes who can slow images down, speed them up, or even reverse them are exhibiting good control.

To create reality in the mind, athletes must concentrate on imaging the behavior perfectly (Weinberg, 1984). If the image you create is not exact, you will need to reattempt the behavior until you get it right in your mind. This is simply an extension of the perfect practice rule that athletes adhere to when practicing physically.

It is important that the skill, event, or event segment be imaged in its entirety (Weinberg & Gould, 1995). The imagined rehearsal of a triple jump takeoff without the run-up or putting a golf ball without the follow-through is often more of a hindrance than a help. In situations of partial imagery rehearsal, errors may occur at the point of change between the rehearsed and unrehearsed images.

In addition to this, it is important to image not only the entire performance associated with a skill, but also a specific positive outcome. For example, a basketball player imaging free-throws should image the shooting action and the outcome of the shooting action (e.g., the ball banking off the boards into the hoop). Also, it is necessary that the athlete ensures that the outcome imagined is the one desired. Although this may sound obvious, for athletes who have trouble controlling images, getting the right outcome imaged is not always a foregone conclusion. For an image to be effective, it is necessary that the outcome matches what the athlete wishes to achieve (Woolfolk, Parrish, & Murphy, 1985).

Because we are attempting to create reality in the mind, the time you take to image an event should parallel the time it would take to physically complete the event (Nideffer, 1985). That is, if it takes a hockey player 15 seconds to skate a full circuit of the rink, it should take that amount of time to image the same event in the mind. A timing test such as this provides a crude measure of how well an image is matching reality.

We can classify images into two distinct categories—internal and external (Mahoney & Avener, 1977). Images that involve seeing or feeling the behavior from the perspective of the individual are known as internal images. Individuals using an internal focus see things just as if they were doing the activity (i.e., through their own eyes). Individuals using an external perspective view the image from an outsider's perspective (i.e., viewing their performance from the stands). Although these two viewpoints do exist, studies have not been able to determine conclusively which is better. However, it appears as if good performers often use both perspectives when imaging a skill or routine, flipping back and forth between the two when appropriate. For example, a gymnast imaging a floor routine might image the run-up internally, flipping to an external perspective to image the back handspring portion.

Weinberg and Gould (1995) have suggested that, in starting to practice and develop imagery skills, the individual should achieve a state of relaxed attention, with no distractions present in the environment. This relaxed state of attention facilitates all the senses during imagery. After practicing and developing imagery skills, the individual will be able to use imagery even when many distractions are present, such as those in a competitive sport environment (i.e., track meets, basketball games, and so forth). Eventually, as imagery skills develop, those distractions will not interfere with the ability to use motor imagery.

The learning experience will give you an opportunity to practice imagery.

Learning Experience

Purpose

To investigate the effects of practice on developing imagery skill.

Measuring Tools

Pretraining and Posttraining Sport Imagery Assessment Questionnaires on pages 145 and 146.

Procedure

1. Choose a partner and take him or her through the progressive relaxation technique (see page 136), or have your partner achieve a relaxed state of attention on his or her own.

2. Take your partner through the imagery assessment exercises that follow this procedure section, and fill out parts of the Pretraining Sport Imagery Assessment Questionnaire as indicated on page 145.

3. Then, lead your partner through the set of four exercises beginning on page 143, which are designed to help develop vivid and controlled images.

4. Practice each exercise on your own, once a day, for 5 days.

5. Following the last practice session, complete the Posttraining Sport Imagery Assessment Questionnaire.

Imagery Assessment Exercises

Conduct this lab experience in a nondistracting environment. If your partner cannot reach a relaxed state, have him or her recline and take him or her through the relaxation sequence (see Experience 14, Physical Relaxation). Guide the imagery assessment exercises by reading the following directions:

"Using an internal focus, see yourself alone, practicing your sport skill." (pause)

"See the situation as if you were practicing your sport—in the gym, or pool, or on a field. Notice the detail of the surroundings; notice the colors and the smells." (pause)

"See yourself begin to practice by yourself. You're all alone practicing." (pause)

"Hear the sounds as you practice—the bounce of the ball, splash of the water, feet hitting the ground, or your own breathing." (pause)

"Focus on what you feel in your body as you go through the movements of your skill. Feel muscles contract and stretch as you move." (pause)

"Notice your emotional feelings, also." (pause)

   Stop and have your partner fill out the first imagery assessment, practicing alone, on the Pretraining Sport Imagery Assessment Questionnaire on page 145. Then, have your partner relax again and take him or her through the second exercise by continuing to read.

"Now, using an internal focus, see yourself competing in your sport." (pause)

"As you see yourself in this situation, hear the sounds around you as you are playing or competing." (pause)

"Feel the movements your body makes and the motions you go through as you compete." (pause)

Stop and have your partner fill out the second imagery assessment, playing in a contest, on the questionnaire and complete the scoring portion according to the directions. Now you are ready to take your partner through the exercises for developing imagery that he or she will practice each day for one week.

Exercises for Developing Imagery

Have your partner lie down and become relaxed. Hold an object in your hand that your partner will be able to see, and read the following directions:

Exercise 1

"Open your eyes and focus on every detail of this object; look at the shape and color." (pause)

"Close your eyes and imagine you are still looking at the object. See all the detail and the colors." (pause)

"Now, open your eyes and compare your image with the real object." (pause)

"Close your eyes again and see the object with its color and detail." (pause)

Exercise 2

"Now, imagine your house. You are standing in the front yard looking at your house; notice the color and the detail." (pause)

"Walk to the front door. Notice how the house seems to grow larger as you get closer." (pause)

"Open the door and walk into your house, and walk to the doorway of your room." (pause)

"Notice all the details as you look around your room." (pause)

"Now, turn around and walk to the front door of your house." (pause)

"Open the door and walk out into the yard. Turn around and look at your house." (pause)

Exercise 3

"Make your house get larger; make it grow bigger in size." (pause)

"Now, make your house get smaller and shrink back to its normal size." (pause)

"Make your house shrink smaller until it is one-half its regular size." (pause)

"Now, make your house get bigger, back to its normal size." (pause)

Exercise 4

"Now, see a beautiful, warm summer day and you standing on a beach." (pause)

"Lie down on the beach and feel the warm sand you are lying on and the penetrating warmth of the sun as you lie quietly." (pause)

"Hear the ocean waves as they break on shore and feel a slight, cool breeze blow over you as you lie on the sand. You feel warm and relaxed." (pause)

"Imagine the blue sky with white clouds." (pause)

"You feel warm and relaxed." (pause)

"Now, open your eyes and sit up, slowly."

Analysis of Results

1. Did your ability to control the images change after the practice sessions?
2. Did your ability to image vividly change with practice?
3. Were any imagery exercises more difficult than others? Which ones? Why?
4. Could you identify all the senses that were operating during the imagery exercises?

Discussion Questions

1. Do your scores indicate that practice influences imagery skill?
2. What implications do your findings have for research using imagery in sport?
3. Do your results indicate a relationship among the sensory dimensions?
4. Do you feel that imagery might be useful for you in sport? Why?

References

Jacobson, E. (1930). Electrical measurements of neuromuscular states during mental activities. Imagination of movement involving skeletal muscles. *American Journal of Physiology, 91,* 547-608.

Mahoney, M.J., & Avener, M. (1977). Psychology of the elite athlete: An exploratory study. *Cognitive Therapy and Research, 1,* 135-141.

Martens, R. (1980). *Psychological skills training for athletes.* Unpublished manuscript, University of Illinois, Urbana-Champaign.

Murphy, S.M., & Jowdy, D.P. (1992). Imagery and mental practice. In T.S. Horn (Ed.), *Advances in sport psychology* (pp. 221-250). Champaign, IL: Human Kinetics.

Nideffer, R.M. (1985). *Athlete's guide to mental training.* Champaign, IL: Human Kinetics.

Orlick, T., & Partington, J. (1988). Mental links to excellence. *The Sport Psychologist, 2,* 105-131.

Richardson, A. (1967). Mental practice: A review and discussion. *Research Quarterly, 38,* 95-107.

Ryan, E.D., & Simons, J. (1982). Efficacy of mental imagery in enhancing mental rehearsal of motor skills. *Journal of Sport Psychology, 4,* 41-51.

Weinberg, R.S. (1984). Mental preparation strategies. In J. Silva & R.S. Weinberg (Eds.), *Psychological foundations of sport* (pp. 145-156). Champaign, IL: Human Kinetics.

Weinberg, R.S., & Gould, D. (1995). *Foundations of sport and exercise psychology.* Champaign, IL: Human Kinetics.

Woolfolk, R.L., Parrish, M.W., & Murphy, S.M. (1985). The effects of positive and negative imagery on motor skill performance. *Cognitive Therapy and Research, 9,* 335-341.

Pretraining Sport Imagery Assessment Questionnaire

This exercise measures your present imagery skill as it pertains to sport participation. Descriptions for two sport situations will be read to you—first, practicing alone, then, playing in a contest. You are to imagine the situations and provide as much detail from your imagination as possible to make the image as real as you can. Then you will rate your imagery on four dimensions:

1. How vividly you saw the image.
2. How clearly you heard the sounds.
3. How vividly you felt the body movements.
4. How clearly you felt the mood or emotion of the situation.

As you listen to each description, think of a specific example in which you are involved—the skill, other people involved, the place, the time, and so forth. Remember that imagery is more than visualizing. Try to involve all the senses.

The rating system is keyed as follows:

1 = very clear and vivid image

2 = moderately clear and vivid image

3 = not clear or vivid, but recognizable image

4 = vague image

5 = no image present

The scale was adapted from one developed by Martens (1980).

Assessment

Practicing alone (circle the appropriate rating)

1.	Rate how well you saw yourself in this situation.	1	2	3	4	5
2.	Rate how well you heard the sounds of doing the activity.	1	2	3	4	5
3.	Rate how well you felt yourself making the movements.	1	2	3	4	5
4.	Rate how well you were aware of your mood and emotions.	1	2	3	4	5

Playing in a contest (circle the appropriate rating)

1.	Rate how well you saw yourself in this situation.	1	2	3	4	5
2.	Rate how well you heard the sounds of doing the activity.	1	2	3	4	5
3.	Rate how well you felt yourself making the movements.	1	2	3	4	5
4.	Rate how well you were aware of your mood and emotions.	1	2	3	4	5

Posttraining Sport Imagery Assessment Questionnaire

This exercise measures your present imagery skill as it pertains to sport participation. Descriptions for two sport situations will be read to you—first, practicing alone, then, playing in a contest. You are to imagine the situations and provide as much detail from your imagination as possible to make the image as real as you can. Then you will rate your imagery on four dimensions:

1.   How vividly you saw the image.
2.   How clearly you heard the sounds.
3.   How vividly you felt the body movements.
4.   How clearly you felt the mood or emotion of the situation.

As you listen to each description, think of a specific example in which you are involved—the skill, other people involved, the place, the time, and so forth. Remember that imagery is more than visualizing—try to involve all the senses.

The rating system is keyed as follows:

1 = very clear and vivid image

2 = moderately clear and vivid image

3 = not clear or vivid, but recognizable image

4 = vague image

5 = no image present

The scale was adapted from one developed by Martens (1980).

Assessment

Practicing alone (circle the appropriate rating)

1.	Rate how well you saw yourself in this situation.	1	2	3	4	5
2.	Rate how well you heard the sounds of doing the activity.	1	2	3	4	5
3.	Rate how well you felt yourself making the movements.	1	2	3	4	5
4.	Rate how well you were aware of your mood and emotions.	1	2	3	4	5

Playing in a contest (circle the appropriate rating)

1.	Rate how well you saw yourself in this situation.	1	2	3	4	5
2.	Rate how well you heard the sounds of doing the activity.	1	2	3	4	5
3.	Rate how well you felt yourself making the movements.	1	2	3	4	5
4.	Rate how well you were aware of your mood and emotions.	1	2	3	4	5

Scoring

Sum the ratings for both of your answers to 1, then both of your answers to 2, and so on, recording them in the proper space below. Total the scores for the four rating dimensions and record the total.

Dimension	Score
1. Visual	_____
2. Auditory	_____
3. Kinesthetic	_____
4. Mood	_____
Total	_____

EXPERIENCE 16

MENTAL PREPARATION

The relationship between cognitive factors and athletic performance has received much attention in sport psychology in recent years. Athletes are trying to get a competitive advantage wherever they can. So, researchers have begun to examine the role that specific cognitive strategies play in improving motor performance. This question of whether athletes can psych themselves up to perform better falls within the topic of mental preparation.

Objectives

In this learning experience, you will learn

- the effects of psyching up on different types of motor tasks, and
- the types of mental preparation strategies athletes use.

Then you will have the opportunity to examine the influence of mental preparation strategies on strength performance.

Basic Considerations

When examining how athletes psych themselves up, research studies have examined several mental preparation strategies, including attentional focus, preparatory arousal, imagery, and self-confidence (Murphy & Jowdy, 1992). Shelton and Mahoney (1978) conducted the first study specifically aimed at determining the content and effects of cognitive strategies on strength performance. Weightlifting subjects were instructed either to psych up (i.e., mentally prepare) or to count backward before squeezing a hand dynamometer. They found that the mental preparation group improved strength, whereas the other group either did not improve or showed decreases in strength. In terms of the content of the mental preparation strategies, the weightlifters reported using a variety of strategies, including imagery, preparatory arousal, self-statements of competence, and attentional focus.

In a similar vein, Weinberg, Gould, and Jackson (1980) conducted an experiment to determine the effects of mental preparation on the performance of three motor tasks involving strength, speed, and balance. They found that effects of mental preparation were task specific. Only in the strength task (i.e., isokinetic leg strength) was performance facilitated by the cognitive techniques. Mental preparation strategies had no influence on the speed-of-arm movement task or on the stabilometer balance task. In terms of mental preparation strategies, the three reported most frequently included attentional focus, imagery, and preparatory arousal.

The results of these laboratory findings also have been extended to a field setting involving track athletes (Caudill, Weinberg, & Jackson, 1983). Sprinters and hurdlers in the mental-preparation condition exhibited significantly better performance in their events than individuals in either an attention-placebo group or a control group. The athletes were consistent in the strategies they employed. The strategies used most often included preparatory arousal, imagery, self-statements of competence, attentional focus, relaxation distraction, and a strategy termed religious beliefs. Some combination of these techniques was employed by 40% of the athletes.

In these studies, individuals used their preferred psyching up strategies before performance. Although the results of these studies suggest that some form of psyching up works, they do not provide any evidence as to which strategies might be most effective. Fortunately, a number of studies have been conducted that require the participants to employ a specific psyching-up technique before performing. In one of the first examples of this, Gould, Weinberg, and Jackson (1980) conducted two studies to determine if different mental preparation strategies produced differential strength performance. The results indicated that two strategies, preparatory arousal and imagery, had the greatest effect on strength performance when compared with the control conditions (i.e., control-rest condition and a counting backward cognitive-distraction condition). Of the two, preparatory arousal was a more consistent strategy in increasing performance.

Tynes and McFatter (1987) had experienced weightlifters perform a task under one of four mental preparation strategies (e.g., self-confidence, imagery, attentional focus, or preparatory arousal) and two control conditions. The results revealed that individuals performed the task significantly better when they mentally prepared than when they did not prepare. In terms of which mental preparation strategy was most effective, the researchers found that the preparatory arousal condition was more effective than the other three preparation conditions.

In another sport-related study, Saintsing and Richman (1988) examined the effects of three cognitive strategies on long-distance running. The results revealed that individuals who received associative task-specific instructions recorded significant improvements in running times versus a control group. Individuals receiving dissociative and psyching up instructions were no more effective in improving running times than were the control group.

Finally, Lee (1990) examined the use of imagery as a psych-up strategy on a muscular endurance task. The premise of the study was to determine whether it is the imaging of a task that is crucial or simply the positive aspects of the mental image that influence performance. To this end, individuals used task-relevant imagery (i.e., image doing the specific task well), task-irrelevant imagery (i.e., image a situation in which you felt happy and confident), or a distraction-control procedure (i.e., counting backwards) before performing muscular endurance tasks. The results for two muscular endurance tasks revealed that the task-relevant imagery group improved significantly more than the other two groups. The results from this preliminary study suggested that the content of the image was crucial in determining the effects on endurance performance. Further, the effects do not appear to depend on alterations in mood state, but rather may operate through cognitive preparation.

Although studies conducted to date have consistently shown a positive relationship between mental preparation strategies and performance (especially strength), many questions are still unanswered. As examples, can we generalize these findings to other athletes and their specific skills (i.e., basketball players, high jumpers, golfers, and so forth)? Does training in a specific mental preparation strategy facilitate performance? Which combination of mental preparation skills works best? Future research needs to address these issues in both the laboratory and field settings.

The learning experience provides you with the opportunity to examine the effects of mental preparation strategies on strength performance.

Learning Experience

Purpose

To observe the influence of mental-preparation strategies on performance in a strength task.

Measuring Tool

A hand dynamometer and the Mental Preparation Data Sheet on page 154.

The Task

1. Measure grip strength in this study using a hand dynamometer.
2. The subject should stand with feet shoulder-width apart.
3. Both arms should be straight and down at the sides.
4. The subject uses his or her dominant hand.
5. The objective is to squeeze the dynamometer as hard as possible.

Procedure

1. Find 10 individuals who are willing to participate in an experiment.
2. Randomly divide the 10 subjects into 2 groups.
3. Designate one group as the control and the other as the experimental group.
4. Demonstrate how to use the dynamometer to each subject.
5. Tell the subjects that they will each do 3 trials.
6. Each subject in both groups performs the task alone, with only the experimenter present to record the scores.
7. Before each trial, give the subjects in the 2 groups their respective instructions orally.
8. Give the following instructions to the control group (counting backward):

"You will have a 20-second interval before each trial during which time I would like you to count backward from 100 by 2s out loud. When the 20 seconds are up, I will say 'go' and I want you to perform to the best of your ability when you are ready. Start counting now."

9. Give the following instructions to the experimental group (preparatory arousal):

"You will have a 20-second interval before each trial during which time I would like you to psych yourself up. Psych yourself up by getting aroused, mad, by screaming; or emotionally charging up by making yourself angry; or motivated by thinking of a situation that makes you angry or motivated. When the 20 seconds are up, I will say 'go' and I want you to perform to the best of your ability when you are ready. I will give you 5 seconds to think of a situation or a strategy to psych yourself up." (Pause for 5 seconds.) "Start psyching up now."

Instruct each subject not to tell anyone what has occurred until everyone has been tested.

Analysis of Results

1. Complete the Mental Preparation Data Sheet.

2. Complete a *t*-test to determine whether a significant difference exists between the means of the two groups.

Discussion Questions

1. What does the *t*-statistic reveal in this experience?

2. Does the data you collected support previous research in this area? If your results are different, can you explain the difference?

3. What other mental preparation strategies could you suggest to increase strength performance?

4. How effective do you think the strategy used in this experience would be in tasks requiring speed? Balance?

5. What would you suggest that an athlete who relies primarily on strength do in the few minutes before his or her event? Why?

References

Caudill, D., Weinberg, R.S., & Jackson, A. (1983). Psyching-up and track athletes: A preliminary investigation. *Journal of Sport Psychology, 5,* 231-235.

Gould, D., Weinberg, R.S., & Jackson, A. (1980). Mental preparation strategies, cognitions and strength performance. *Journal of Sport Psychology, 2,* 329-339.

Lee, C. (1990). Psyching up for a muscular endurance task: Effects of image content on performance and mood state. *Journal of Sport & Exercise Psychology, 12,* 66-73.

Murphy, S.M., & Jowdy, D.P. (1992). Imagery and mental practice. In T.S. Horn (Ed.), *Advances in sport psychology* (pp. 221-250). Champaign, IL: Human Kinetics.

Saintsing, D.E., & Richman, C.L. (1988). Effects of three cognitive strategies on long-distance running. *Bulletin of the Psychonomic Society, 26,* 34-36.

Shelton, A.O., & Mahoney, M.J. (1978). The content and effect of psyching-up strategies in weightlifters. *Cognitive Therapy and Research, 2,* 275-284.

Tynes, L.L., & McFatter, R.M. (1987). The efficacy of "psyching" strategies on a weight-lifting task. *Cognitive Therapy and Research, 11,* 327-336.

Weinberg, R.S., Gould, D., & Jackson, A. (1980). Cognition and motor performance: Effect of psyching-up strategies on three motor tasks. *Cognitive Therapy and Research, 4,* 239-245.

Mental Preparation Data Sheet

Control group					Experimental group				
	Strength score					Strength score			
Subject	T1	T2	T3	$\bar{X}$	Subject	T1	T2	T3	$\bar{X}$
1					6				
2					7				
3					8				
4					9				
5					10				

To calculate the *t*-statistic use

$$t = \frac{\bar{X}_1 - \bar{X}_2}{\sqrt{\dfrac{S_1^2}{N_1} + \dfrac{S_2^2}{N_2}}}$$

EXPERIENCE 17

ATTENTION

What do the following three examples have in common?

    i.   You are walking down a familiar hallway thinking about what you need to do before retiring for the night when you bump into a wall that you have bypassed successfully many times before.

    ii.   A quarterback has a pass picked as he throws into double coverage, when 10 yards to his right he had a receiver wide open waving his hands for the ball.

    iii.   A young soccer player streaking down the field with two teammates passes the ball to his father after he hears his father shout from the sidelines, "Pass it, pass it."

Although these three scenarios may share other commonalities (e.g., like embarrassment), one thing they have in common is that they all deal with an individual's attentional focus. Considering the myriad of stimuli that each of us experiences constantly, life would be difficult without selective attention. As the last two examples illustrate, sport is no different. In fact, there are few factors more important to performing optimally in sport than the ability to focus on the appropriate cues (Boutcher, 1992; Nideffer, 1976). Whether an individual is learning or performing in a sport setting, attention to the most appropriate cues is a critical variable. Although the importance of attentional factors in sport performance has long been recognized by athletes and coaches, only in recent years have researchers begun to investigate the nature of the attention-performance relationship.

Objectives

In this learning experience you will learn

- what is meant by the term attention,
- the types of attentional focus athletes use,

- the use of a scale to measure attentional style,
- the typical attentional strategies long-distance runners use, and
- the relationship between attention and arousal.

Then you will have the opportunity to test the effects of selected attentional strategies.

Basic Considerations

Attention is the term that describes the process whereby an individual uses his or her senses to perceive the external world. Focusing your attention simply involves becoming aware of one thing to the exclusion of others. To illustrate this process, focus on your hamstring muscles as you sit reading this book (assuming that you are sitting). Notice the points where your muscles touch the chair and identify how much pressure you feel at these points. What you have done is become aware of these pressure points, while excluding the other stimuli within your immediate environment—a personal example of attention in action.

In sport, two types of attentional focus were initially identified as being important for performance—width (broad-narrow) and direction (internal-external) (Nideffer, 1976, 1981) (see figure 17.1). According to Nideffer, width was concerned with how much information, and how broad a perceptual field, an athlete tried to deal with at any time. For example, an athlete who must attend to many pieces of information, such as a basketball player looking for a teammate to pass to, needs a broad focus. On the other hand, an archer focusing on the center of a single target would require a narrow focus of attention. Also, shifting from narrow to broad or broad to narrow often occurs. A hockey player scans the ice for an open teammate (broad focus); when he locates one, he focuses in on that individual for the pass (narrow focus).

The other dimension of attention involves direction of focus, which can be internal or external to the athlete. By focusing on his or her own thoughts, feelings, or internal cues, an athlete is adopting an internal focus. By focusing on environmental cues, the play, and strategies of the opponent, an athlete is adopting an external focus. An athlete watching a ball game must have an external focus, whereas an individual anticipating an opponent's next move must have an internal focus. Similar to the width dimension, an athlete must be able to shift attention between an internal and external focus.

Nideffer (1976) has proposed further that individuals may possess a specific attentional style that interacts with the attentional demands inherent in a sporting situation. In terms of attentional demands, Nideffer (1976) suggested that there are four types that may arise in any given sporting situation—broad internal, broad external, narrow internal, and narrow external. According to Nideffer (1976), optimal performance will result when the attentional demands specific to the situation match the individual's attentional style.

To assess these individual attentional styles, Nideffer (1976) developed a questionnaire titled the Test of Attentional and Interpersonal Style (TAIS). It measures attentional abilities (not sport specific) varying in width (broad-narrow) and direction (internal-external) of focus. Although the TAIS has 17 subscales, only 6 measure attentional processes. The 6 attentional subscales are as follows: broad external, broad internal, narrow attentional focus, reduced attentional focus, external overload, and internal overload. The first three subscales assess effective use of attention, whereas the latter three assess inappropriate attentional styles.

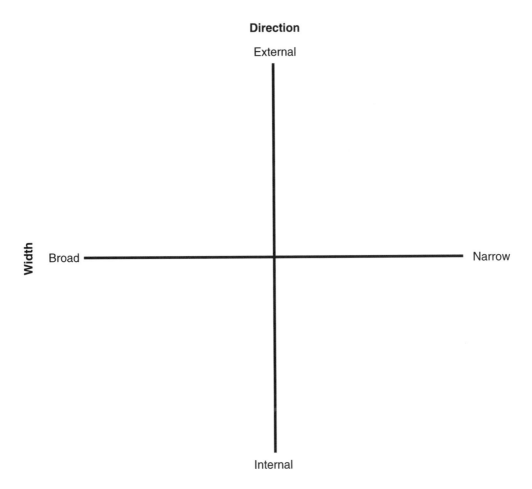

Direction

External

Internal

Width

Broad ———————————————— Narrow

Figure 17.1 Nideffer's types of attentional focus.

Although the TAIS attentional subscales have intuitive appeal, research in the sport setting has found support for only the width dimension, not the direction dimension (Summers, Miller, & Ford, 1991). Further, some research suggests that the width component of attention has two dimensions—scanning and focusing. Scanning refers to the amount of movement that occurs while attending, and focusing refers to the width of the scan (Summers, Miller, & Ford, 1991; Vallerand, 1983). These studies suggest that width may be a more important component than direction; however, a definitive conclusion awaits further research.

In terms of predicting sport performance, the TAIS has not fared much better. Although several studies have found an expected relationship between the subscales of TAIS and sport performance (e.g., Albrecht & Feltz, 1987), several others have failed to find any meaningful relationship (e.g., Vallerand, 1983). In attempting to increase its predictive power, several investigators have developed sport-specific versions of the TAIS. Although these sport-specific measures have fared better in predicting sport performance, the results are still equivocal (Albrecht & Feltz, 1987; Summers, Miller, & Ford, 1991). Future studies will need to investigate whether attentional style is sport specific, whether a general sport measure may be more valid than the present TAIS, or whether TAIS in its present form is valid for sport settings.

Another aspect of attentional style that has surfaced over the years concerns the attentional styles marathon runners use. In past research using long-distance runners, two types of attentional focus have been identified—disassociators and associators. Some long-distance runners use the disassociation attentional strategy to overcome the pain barrier by focusing attention elsewhere (Morgan & Pollock, 1977). Quite simply, they disassociate from the pain by attending to other topics. Runners using this technique report doing things that range from performing complex mathematical calculations to writing a letter in their heads during a race. Other runners use the opposite attentional strategy. Rather than disassociating, they associate with the pain and discomfort. These individuals constantly monitor their body signals and keep reminding themselves to "stay loose" or to "relax and not tie up."

In an attempt to explain these findings, researchers have speculated that association allows an individual to monitor his or her body functions and make adjustments to maintain peak efficiency. Disassociation, while probably more pleasant, may distract an individual's attention from the task at hand—running efficiently. Morgan and Pollock (1977) found that these two attentional strategies differentiated elite from nonelite runners, with elite runners preferring associative attentional strategies and nonelite runners preferring to disassociate. Spink and Longhurst (1986) found a similar result using swimmers. In contrast to this finding, Schomer (1986) found that regardless of whether marathon runners were elite or nonelite, an associative attentional strategy increased running speed. Future research needs to address which of these explanations is better.

One other relationship worth mentioning is between arousal and attention. Easterbrook (1959) proposed that as arousal increases, the range of cues that an individual uses to direct his or her behavior becomes restricted, thus limiting performance. Several sport studies examining this relationship have supported Easterbrook's theory. In addition, increases in arousal tend to reduce an individual's ability to shift from one type of attention to another (Nideffer, 1981). In addition to a narrowing and a reduction in shifting ability, increasing arousal results in attention becoming internally focused. Because sports demand an external focus most of the time, this increasing internal focus usually results in what is commonly termed choking (Nideffer, 1981).

Obviously, the investigation of the relationship between attention and performance has important implications for coaches and athletes. Before we can realize the importance of attentional factors in facilitating performance, we need more research to address the issues (i.e., the relationship of arousal to attention and performance). The learning experience that follows enables you to examine the effect of two attentional strategies on strength performance.

Learning Experience

Purpose

To investigate the influence of two attentional strategies on performance of a muscular endurance task.

Measuring Tools

A strong wall, a stopwatch (or a wristwatch), and the Attentional Focus Data Sheet on page 162.

Procedure

1. Select 10 individuals who are willing to help you in an experiment.

2. Randomly divide the subjects into 2 equal groups. Ensure size distribution. It is important to equalize the groups in terms of strength as much as possible.

3. Identify Group 1 as the association group and Group 2 as the disassociation group.

4. Explain and demonstrate the skier's squat to each subject in both groups. (See Experience 6, Social Facilitation, for a description of skier's squat.) Explain to the subjects that the objective of the task is to do their best.

5. Each subject performs the task alone, with only the experimenter present to keep time.

6. Before performing the task, provide the following written instructions (or you may read the instructions to each subject if you wish) to the association and disassociation groups.

Instructions—Association Group

"As you know, the task you are to complete is an endurance exercise. During most endurance tasks, for example, running a marathon or long-distance swimming, you experience a certain amount of discomfort and pain. These decrease your ability to keep going, to put in a maximal effort. Recent research with world-class marathon runners, however, has suggested a technique that may be useful in increasing performance by decreasing the discomfort you experience in an endurance exercise.

This technique involves associating with, or being totally aware of, the discomfort and pain you are experiencing during the exercise, then coping with it using relaxation. During the performance of the endurance exercise, we want you to use this technique. This is how you do it.

After you begin the exercise, concentrate and narrow your attention to only those parts of the body that are feeling tension or discomfort. Focus on the internal feelings of those muscles. Try to relax the muscle as much as you can. As you feel the discomfort increasing, remind yourself to relax. Block out all outside thoughts and concentrate on the internal feelings of your body, and as you feel the discomfort increase take that as the cue to concentrate more deeply on relaxing. Now, get into the skier's squat and we will begin."

Instructions—Disassociation Group

"As you know, the task you are to complete is an endurance exercise. During most endurance tasks, for example, running a marathon or long-distance swimming, you experience a certain amount of discomfort and pain. These decrease your ability to keep going, to put in a maximal effort. Recent research with world-class marathon runners, however, has suggested a technique that may be useful in increasing performance by decreasing the discomfort you experience in an endurance exercise.

This technique involves disassociation, or cutting yourself off, from the sensory feedback you normally receive from your body. This requires you to think about other things to take your mind off any discomfort or pain you may be feeling. During the performance of the endurance exercise, we want you to use this technique. This is how you do it.

Focus your attention on things other than what you are doing by making up a story. Make up a story on any subject you like, think it through, and visualize the scenes as clearly as you can. See every detail, and feel every emotion of this trip you are taking through your mind. You might like to take a holiday with a friend, play a game of squash, do mental arithmetic, or build a house. Make up your own story and images. Now, get into the skier's squat and we will begin."

Analysis of Results

1. Complete the Attentional Focus Data Sheet.
2. Compute a t-test to establish whether a significant difference exists between the two groups.

Discussion Questions

1. Did a difference exist between the groups? Is it significant?
2. Is the difference you found in the correct direction? In other words, did you find what you might have expected?
3. Briefly explain the mechanisms that you think underlie each attentional strategy (association versus disassociation).
4. Which strategy would you prefer to use to get you through a marathon? Why?
5. State three implications that your results might have for individuals involved in endurance activities.

References

Albrecht, R.R., & Feltz, D.L. (1987). Generality and specificity of attention related to competitive anxiety and sport performance. *Journal of Sport Psychology, 9,* 231-248.

Boutcher, S.H. (1992). Attention and athletic performance. An integrated approach. In T.S. Horn (Ed.), *Advances in sport psychology* (pp. 251-266). Champaign, IL: Human Kinetics.

Easterbrook, J.A. (1959). The effect of emotion on cue utilization and the organization of behavior. *Psychological Review, 66,* 182-201.

Morgan, W.P., & Pollock, M.L. (1977). Psychological characterization of the elite distance runner. In P.V. Milvy (Ed.), *Annals of the New York Academy of Science* (pp. 382-403). New York: New York Academy of Science.

Nideffer, R.M. (1976). *The inner athlete*. New York: Crowell.

Nideffer, R.M. (1981). *The ethics and practice of applied sport psychology*. Ithaca, NY: Mouvement.

Schomer, H. (1986). Mental strategies and the perception of effort of marathon runners. *International Journal of Sport Psychology, 17*, 41-59.

Spink, K.S., & Longhurst, K. (1986). Cognitive strategies and swimming performance: An exploratory study. *The Australian Journal of Science and Medicine in Sport, 18*, 4-13.

Summers, J.J., Miller, K., & Ford, S. (1991). Attentional style and basketball performance. *Journal of Sport & Exercise Psychology, 8*, 239-253.

Vallerand, R.J. (1983). Attention and decision-making: A test of the predictive validity of the Test of Attentional and Interpersonal Style (TAIS) in a sport setting. *Journal of Sport Psychology, 5*, 449-459.

Attentional Focus Data Sheet

Association group		Disassociation group	
Subject	Strength score (X_1)	Subject	Strength score (X_2)
1		6	
2		7	
3		8	
4		9	
5		10	

To calculate the *t*-statistic use
$$t = \frac{\overline{X}_1 - \overline{X}_2}{\sqrt{\dfrac{S_1^{\,2}}{N_1} + \dfrac{S_2^{\,2}}{N_2}}}$$

EXPERIENCE 18

ENHANCING MOTIVATION

One recent area to develop in sport psychology is enhancing motivation. A question teachers and coaches continually ask is how to prevent dropouts and enhance the continuance of children, in particular, in the sport experience. One stimulating avenue for intervention programs has come from achievement goal theory and research. Whereas many intervention programs focus on the individual, to enhance worthy attributes (see many of the learning experiences in this section of this book), this approach focuses on the adults who organize and coach participants in sport and physical activity. We focus on the motivational climate the teacher, parent, and coach create.

Objectives

In this learning experience you will learn
- the meaning of mastery and performance motivational climates,
- the research pertaining to performance and mastery motivational climates,
- the criteria for creating different motivational climates, and
- the enhancement of motivation.

Then you will have the opportunity to conduct a field study in the area of motivation and observe the motivational climate in children's competitive sport.

Basic Considerations

This learning experience focuses on motivation as determined by the perceived motivational climate that the individuals in charge of the program create. We assume that these individuals influence the thought processes that affect motivated behavior. The real difference between this learning experience and the one titled Understanding Motivation (experience 11) is that we investigate the situational determinants of motivation, not the dispositional determinants.

This research has examined how the structure of the environment can make it more or less likely that an individual will adopt a particular achievement goal. The premise of research from a situational perspective is that the nature of children's experiences and how they interpret them influence the degree to which task and ego involvement is salient within the context. We assume this affects the achievement behaviors of children so they choose adaptive achievement strategies (namely to work hard, seek challenging tasks, persist in the face of difficulty) in task-involving situations and maladaptive achievement strategies (namely to seek easy tasks, reduce effort, or give up in the face of difficulty) in ego-involving situations (see Ames, 1992). If the physical activity context is characterized by interpersonal competition, social comparison, the coach or teacher emphasizing outcomes and winning, and public recognition of demonstrated ability, a *performance climate* exists, and individuals are likely to be ego involved. If, on the other hand, the situation is characterized by learning and mastering skills, trying hard and doing your best, and the coach or teacher using private feedback about demonstrated ability, a *mastery climate* exists, and individuals are likely to be task involved.

Papaioannou (1995) has reported findings in a physical education setting showing that when the students perceived a high task involvement and a low ego involvement, they attributed success to effort and not ability. Also, regardless of perceived ability, the perception of high task involvement was a strong predictor of motivation in physical education, for example, intrinsic motivation, interest in the lesson, importance of the lesson, behavioral control, intentions for high effort, and intentions for participation in all physical education classes. In contrast, perceptions of high ego involvement were either negatively related or unrelated to motivational indices.

Enhancing Motivation

The issue remains, however, of how to enhance the students' motivation in sport and physical education. Although individually affecting change in a child's dispositional orientation may be effective, individual change is not practical in most educational contexts. We need to develop strategies to determine how to most effectively enhance motivation and adaptive achievement behaviors. A growing body of literature suggests that the teacher plays an active role in constructing children's perceptions of the motivational climate and, consequently, the quality of their motivation (see Epstein, 1989). Most researchers have suggested that we develop strategies and instructional practices that help the teacher to create a task-involving motivational climate (Ames, 1992; Roberts & Treasure, 1992).

Epstein (1989) has argued that features of achievement influence a wide range of motivational processes. These structural features are interdependent and when taken together define the motivational climate. She coined the acronym TARGET to represent the Task, Authority, Reward, Grouping, Evaluation, and Timing structures of the achievement context. She contends that how the teacher or coach structures the context greatly determines whether a child will perceive the context as task or ego involving. Researchers have conducted few studies in a physical education or sport context to manipulate the motivational climate. Adopting Epstein's (1989) approach, Treasure and Roberts (1995) hypothesized that by manipulating the physical education context to be strongly task or ego involving, children's perceptions of the motivational climate would predict their cognitive and affective responses. This study focused on teaching basic soccer skills and took place during 10 successive sessions of the participants' daily physical education class. This study initially involved identifying strategies that promote either an ego or task achievement goal in a physical education setting and organizing these strategies into Epstein's six TARGET areas. Each strategy was then operationalized for specific instructional practices to help the teacher implement the strategies. The intervention model allowed the researchers to compare an ego-involving motivational climate with a task-involving motivational climate.

The findings clearly demonstrated that those children in the ego-treatment condition perceived the motivational climate to be ego involving, and those who participated in the task condition perceived a task-involving motivational climate. The results demonstrated that by manipulating the TARGET structures of the achievement context, a physical education teacher can affect the motivational climate enough to override the dispositional goal orientations of students. This is a significant finding. By manipulating the TARGET structures of the context, a teacher can foster a particular achievement goal and play an active role in constructing a child's physical education experience. The children in the task-treatment condition indicated that they preferred to engage in more challenging tasks, believed success was the result of motivation and effort, and experienced more satisfaction with the activity than children in the ego-treatment condition. Children who participated in the ego-treatment condition, however, reported that deception was a key to success.

It has been suggested that fostering task involvement may be challenging in the context of physical activity, as competition is inherent in the activity (Duda, 1992). The results of this study, however, suggest that in a short time, a teacher can structure a physical education context that influences a child's recognition of a task-involving motivational climate and significantly enhance her or his quality of motivation. From a motivational perspective, Treasure and Roberts (1995) clearly demonstrate not only that it is possible to create a task-involving climate, but also that children thrive in such a context. Task involvement enhances motivation within physical education. Based on these findings, Treasure and Roberts suggested some strategies that a physical educator could use to foster task involvement and enhance the quality of children's motivation in physical education. We shall address each Epstein (1989) TARGET structure in turn.

Task

A central element of any achievement context is the design of tasks and learning activities. Embedded in tasks is information that children use to make judgments about their ability, willingness to apply effort, and feelings of satisfaction. Research has demonstrated that tasks involving variety and diversity are more likely than tasks that involve turn-taking where the whole class is doing the same skill to facilitate an interest in learning and task involvement (e.g., Nicholls, 1989). To enhance task involvement, therefore, individuals should engage in different tasks and have different assignments. With this, students develop a sense of their own ability that is not dependent on social comparison. For example, during a basketball class students should have a choice of size of ball to use, and the teacher should set different tasks for the students depending on their level of development.

Authority

Responsibility in the learning situation relates to the degree that teachers involve children in decision making, and influences adaptive or positive motivation patterns in children (Ames, 1992). Evidence suggests that children's feelings of perceived ability are higher in classrooms in which the teacher and student share the decision-making process. Therefore, to enhance task involvement students should participate actively in the learning process by choosing the tasks they want to learn; set up equipment and tests; and monitor and evaluate their own and, when appropriate, the performance of their partner during testing sessions. For example, during a dribbling soccer skills test, students could work together to set up the dribbling course correctly, then monitor the performance of each other by recording times on successive trials using a stopwatch.

Reward

Using rewards and incentives is an obvious aspect of a child's physical education or sport experience. It often seems that rewards and incentives are more important than the activity itself! Although given with good intentions to motivate children, rewards and incentives can have paradoxical and detrimental effects when applied to an entire group of children with varying abilities and levels of interest (see the learning experience titled Intrinsic Motivation). The research evidence from education is considerable, demonstrating the undermining effects of rewards when students perceive them as bribes or as controlling. Perhaps most significantly, because rewards are often public and given differentially, they invite social comparison. When recognition for accomplishment or progress is private between the teacher and the child, feelings of pride and satisfaction are less likely to come from doing better than others and more likely to come from self-referenced perceptions. This fosters a task-involving perception of the motivational climate. Thus, by focusing rewards on individual gains, improvement, and progress, *all* children can develop an appreciation of their abilities. It is vitally important that physical educators recognize that types of rewards, reasons for rewards, and distribution of rewards determine whether children develop feelings of intrinsic satisfaction and continued interest in physical activity.

Grouping

We can structure learning situations so children work competitively, cooperatively, or individually. Each structure has different consequences for children's learning and motivation. When competition or social comparison is emphasized, children focus on their ability and often engage in debilitating self-evaluations and cognitions. In contrast, when children work toward individual goals or within a cooperative structure, they focus more on their effort, and derive benefit from trying hard or working successfully with others (Ames & Ames, 1984). To foster a task-involving motivational climate, therefore, students should work on individual tasks, for example, how many times they can execute a skill in a set time. When individual tasks are impractical, set small group cooperative tasks. During a skill testing session, students could work in pairs, monitoring and recording their own and the performance of their partner on the task. When you desire large group activities, select the groups randomly to ensure that they are heterogeneous in composition.

Evaluation

How children are evaluated is one of the most salient features of any achievement context. The issue is not merely whether children are evaluated, but rather how children perceive the meaning of the evaluative information. Much research suggests that evaluation practices can have deleterious effects on motivation when they are normatively based, public, and linked to ability assessments (e.g., Nicholls, 1989). Evaluation systems that emphasize social comparison and normative standards of performance evoke ego involvement, which focuses children on evaluating their ability compared with their peers. As a consequence, children's self-worth, level of intrinsic interest, and perceived ability are impaired.

We must emphasize, however, that the mere availability of social comparison information is not problematic. Rather, it is emphasizing it that undermines the linkages between effort, outcome, and affect. This would be an important point when we consider the pervasiveness of social comparative information within physical education and sport competition. In contrast, when evaluation is self-referenced and based on personal improvement, progress toward individual goals, participation, and effort, children are more likely to be task involved. Children focus on their effort, rather than ability, and use specific task strategies that will contribute to improvement and skill mastery. To facilitate task involvement in physical education and sport, therefore, evaluation should involve multiple, private self-tests that base assessment on effort and personal improvement. For example, when practicing a skill, you would ask a student to see how many times he or she could perform the required skill in a set time and record the number in a log.

Timing

Research from education has indicated that the pace of instruction and the time allotted for completing tasks significantly influences children's motivation. Given the effect of physical and psychological maturation on performance in physical activity during childhood and adolescence, the issue of time would appear to be as critical, if not more so, as in the classroom. To foster task involvement in physical education and sport, therefore, a teacher must consider the interaction between time and the task design (e.g., how much children are asked to accomplish within specific time periods), authority (e.g., whether children are allowed to schedule the rate, order, or completion time of tasks), grouping (e.g., whether quality of instructional time is equitable across groups), and evaluation (e.g., time pressure on performance) structure of the achievement context.

Research from an achievement goal perspective suggests that to enhance adaptive achievement striving in sport and physical education, adults should focus on personal improvement and effort rather than on immediate normative performance. To this end, researchers believe the instructional practices and strategies we have discussed may assist efforts to construct task-involving physical activity contexts.

Learning Experience

Purpose

To observe the motivational climate a coach creates in a children's competitive sport program.

Measuring Tool

The Coach Motivational Climate Assessment Scale on page 169.

Procedure

1. Select any competitive activity for children that involves one or more coaches.

2. Select one coach to observe.

3. Using the scale on page 169, assess the coach on all the categories shown.

Analysis of Results

Write an evaluation of the coach from a motivational point of view. Do you think the coach created a mastery environment, a performance environment, or a combination? Was he or she a good coach for the age of the participants? How much fun were the children having?

Discussion Questions

1. Was this the kind of coach you would want to send your children to?
2. Were any one or two of the six categories more important than the others in creating the climate observed?
3. What kind of a motivational climate do children seem to need from a motivational point of view? Why?
4. What are the implications of your observation for children's sport in general?
5. Would you suggest anything to change in children's sport based on your observations?

References

Ames, C. (1992). Achievement goals and the classroom climate. In J. Meece & D. Schunk (Eds.), *Student perceptions in the classroom* (pp.327-348). Hillsdale, NJ: Erlbaum.

Ames, C., & Ames R. (Eds.) (1984). *Research on motivation in education* (Vol. 1). New York: Academic Press.

Duda, J. (1992). Motivation in sport settings. An achievement goal perspective. In G.C. Roberts (Ed.), *Motivation in exercise and sport* (pp. 57-92). Champaign, IL: Human Kinetics.

Epstein, J. (1989). Family structures and students motivation: A developmental perspective. In C. Ames & R. Ames (Eds.), *Research on motivation in education* (Vol.3, pp. 259-295). New York: Academic Press.

Nicholls, J. (1989). *The competitive ethos and democratic education.* Cambridge, MA: Harvard University Press.

Papaioannou, A. (1995). Motivation and goal perspectives in children's physical education. In S.J.H. Biddle (Ed.), *European perspectives on exercise and sport psychology* (pp. 245-269). Champaign, IL: Human Kinetics.

Roberts, G.C., & Treasure, D.C. (1992). Children in sport. *Sport Science Review, 2,* 46-64.

Treasure, D.C., & Roberts, G.C. (1995). Applications of achievement goal theory to physical education: Implications for enhancing motivation. *Quest, 47,* 475-489.

Coach Motivational Climate Assessment Scale

	Strongly agree				Strongly disagree
Task design—How did the coach design the task for the participants?					
The participants had lots of flexibility.	1	2	3	4	5
The participants had lots of choice.	1	2	3	4	5
Authority—How did the coach use his or her authority?					
The coach always directed activity publicly.	1	2	3	4	5
The coach talked individually to the participants.	1	2	3	4	5
Recognition—How did the coach recognize the participants?					
The coach made public assessments of athletes.	1	2	3	4	5
The coach made private comments to the athletes.	1	2	3	4	5
Grouping—How did the coach organize the athletes?					
All grouping was according to ability.	1	2	3	4	5
Grouping was heterogeneous.	1	2	3	4	5
Evaluation—How did the coach evaluate the athletes?					
The coach compared athletes with one another.	1	2	3	4	5
The coach gave private evaluations.	1	2	3	4	5
Timing—How did the coach organize the timing of practices?					
Everyone did the same task at the same time.	1	2	3	4	5
Athletes chose how long they practiced.	1	2	3	4	5

EXPERIENCE 19

LEADERSHIP

What do the following three people have in common—Indira Ghandi, Michael Jordan, and Vince Lombardi? Although several characteristics may come to mind, I am certain that one common response would be leadership. Leadership is a perplexing phenomena in life. Most of us acknowledge its importance. Most of us can identify leaders from lists of individuals that we see, as we did here. Also, most of us can come up with our own shining examples of leaders, usually with little or no prompting. Yet, when we look at the scientific literature, there is little understanding of what a leader is or what characteristics separate successful leaders from less successful leaders.

Objectives

In this learning experience you will learn

- a definition of leadership,
- two approaches to studying leadership in the physical activity setting, and
- the effect of coaches' expectations on athlete behavior.

Then you will have the opportunity to observe a coach in action to determine whether he or she interacts differently with skilled athletes than with less skilled athletes.

Basic Considerations

In the literature, the idea of what is and is not leadership has not been clarified. However, in its broadest sense, leadership can be conceived as "the behavioral process of influencing individuals and groups toward set goals" (Barrow, 1977, p. 232).

In terms of understanding leadership, there have been numerous approaches advanced throughout the years in the literature. Although leadership is important in the sport setting, it is surprising that research on leadership in this setting is conspicuous by its absence. Although this lack of sport-related studies may be due to several factors, one may be the absence of any theory to explain leadership in the sport setting (Reimer & Chelladurai, 1995). Fortunately, two sport-specific theoretical frameworks have been advanced in recent years to help explain leadership in the sport setting. These include the Mediational Model of Leadership (Smoll & Smith, 1989) and the Multidimensional Model of Leadership (Chelladurai, 1993).

The Mediational Model of Leadership stems from the work of Smoll, Smith, and colleagues (cf. Smoll & Smith, 1989), who examined leadership in the youth sport setting over several years. In the first phase of their research they developed an instrument to assess coaching behaviors called the Coaching Behavior Assessment System (CBAS). This observational instrument consisted of several behavioral categories identified as comprising most coaching behaviors. Further, these coaching behavior categories were separated into two groups—reactive behaviors and spontaneous behaviors. Reactive behaviors were those the coach made in response to athlete and team behaviors. Spontaneous behaviors, on the other hand, were not in reaction to the behavior of team members, but were initiated by the coach alone. The CBAS includes eight kinds of reactive behaviors, which are positive reinforcement, nonreinforcement, mistake-contingent encouragement, mistake-contingent technical instruction, punishment, punitive technical instruction, ignoring mistakes, and keeping control. In addition, there are four spontaneous behaviors monitored in the CBAS, including general technical instruction, general encouragement, organization, and general communication. After extensive testing, the CBAS inventory was found to be a reliable and valid observational instrument.

In the second phase, CBAS was used to determine the relationship between the behaviors of baseball coaches and player perceptions of coaching behaviors, attitudes and satisfaction. The results revealed that coaches evaluated positively and negatively by the young athletes demonstrated distinctly different coaching behaviors. Positively evaluated coaches gave more technical instruction, gave more reinforcement and mistake-contingent feedback, and exhibited more behaviors associated with keeping control. Negatively evaluated coaches, on the other hand, generally were more punitive and gave more punitive technical instruction.

In terms of attitude, researchers found that coaching behaviors accounted for about half the variance in postseason attitudes toward the coach and the sport itself. The strongest predictors of players' liking the coach were the coach's rate of technical instruction in response to mistakes. Keeping control and general encouragement, on the other hand, were negatively related to player's attitude toward the sport.

The results of these studies revealed that certain coaching behaviors were associated with player satisfaction. These included supportive behaviors such as reinforcement and mistake-contingent encouragement. Instructional behaviors, including general technical instruction and mistake-contingent technical instruction, also were noted as important correlates of player satisfaction.

In the final phase (an experimental field study), one group of baseball coaches was trained to coach with a positive approach (consistent with the findings of their previous studies), and a second (control) group received no such instruction. Results showed that the behaviors exhibited by the two groups of coaches differed significantly. The young players exposed to the coaches who were trained to employ positive behaviors demonstrated greater enjoyment, more desire to play, and rated their coaches as more knowledgeable than did players who played for the control (did not receive the training) coaches.

This research by Smoll and Smith and their colleagues is important for at least three reasons. First, it is a sport-specific model addressing leadership. Second, the results suggest a relationship between coaching behaviors and the young player's evaluation of his or her sport experience. Third, the results illustrate that coaches can be trained effectively to relate appropriately to their players. Without doubt, these results give impetus to the coaching training programs now operating in various countries (e.g., Canada—the National Coaching Certification Program; United States—the American Sport Education Program; and Australia—the National Coaching Accreditation Scheme).

A second approach to understanding leadership in the sport setting comes from Chelladurai's Multidimensional Model of Leadership (Chelladurai, 1993). The premise of the model is that the congruence among what leader behaviors are required in the situation, what leader behaviors are preferred by the athletes, and what the leader actually does has a positive effect on athlete satisfaction and group performance. Thus, the model proposes three states of leader behavior—required, preferred, and actual.

Specifics for leader behavior required by the situation consist of those conforming to established norms within the team or organization (e.g., team size, nature of the task, etc.). The second state, leader behavior preferred by the members, are those that the athletes prefer and are based mainly on athlete characteristics such as age, skill level, and psychological characteristics, to name a few. The final leadership state, actual behavior, are those behaviors the leader displays that are influenced by the leader's personal characteristics. Each leadership state also is influenced differentially by antecedent conditions associated with the situation, leader characteristics, and member characteristics. Putting this all together, the model proposes that group outcome and athlete satisfaction will be optimized when leaders engage in behaviors that are preferred by the athletes and consistent with the requirements of the situation.

Using this model of proposed leadership, Chelladurai and his colleagues (Chelladurai & Saleh, 1980) developed an instrument to assess leadership in the sport setting called the Leadership Scale for Sports (LSS). The LSS contains five dimensions of leader behavior. These include training and instruction, social support, positive feedback, autocratic style, and democratic style. Training and instruction consists of coaching behaviors directed at improving the athlete's performance (e.g., emphasizing and facilitating training, clarifying working relationships between players). Social support refers to those coaching behaviors that focus on positive interpersonal relations with athletes, concern for their welfare, and establishing a positive group atmosphere. Positive feedback refers to those behaviors that involve recognizing and rewarding good performance. The final two dimensions refer to the coach's decision-making style. Democratic behavior is those coaching behaviors that allow athletes to participate in decisions about the group (e.g., group goals, practice methods, game strategies). Autocratic behavior, on the other hand, involves independent decision making by the coach and focuses on the coach's personal authority.

The Multidimensional Model of Leadership and the attendant measurement instrument, the LSS, have generated a lot of research interest. For the most part, the studies that researchers have conducted thus far have supported the model. In terms of consequences, increasing athlete satisfaction (Reimer & Chelladurai, 1995) and outcomes (Weiss & Friedrichs, 1986) have been associated with the congruence of actual and preferred leader behaviors.

To this point, the literature discussed has focused on sport exclusively. However, a modified version of the LSS has been used recently to examine leadership in the exercise setting (Spink & Twardochleb, 1996). The preliminary results appear promising in supporting the original structure of the instrument. However, much more work is needed to determine the relationship of the revised version to the original sport instrument.

Another important factor in the coach-athlete interaction concerns expectancies. The coach is often subject to expectancies that may bias his or her observations and behaviors. Quite simply, a coach's expectancies of an athlete often lead to how he or she behaves with the athlete and, subsequently, affect the athlete's performance. Research has documented that teacher's expectancies have resulted in differences in students' performances consistent with those expectancies, even though the students started with equal ability (Rosenthal & Jacobson, 1968). How these expectancies are conveyed include verbal and nonverbal cues that provide the learner with indications about what is expected of him or her.

One important issue about expectancies, and how they are conveyed, is that the coach or teacher is often unaware that he or she is acting any differently toward individuals. This has important practical implications, as research has shown that coaches give varying feedback to athletes who differ in areas such as ability levels (Horn, 1984). To alleviate this problem, Spink (1983) has suggested that coaches monitor their behaviors toward their athletes. If they become aware of their expectancy effects, coaches may adopt strategies to improve their effectiveness by eliminating any problems.

Sport programs for children and youths have been receiving more attention from sport psychology researchers. Although some valuable research has been conducted, much is still to be done. Researchers must provide answers that will improve young athletes' sport participation through improved leadership (i.e., coaching effectiveness). The learning experience gives you the opportunity to see how a coach interacts with his or her athletes.

Learning Experience

Purpose

To observe the behaviors of a coach as he or she interacts with skilled and unskilled athletes.

Measuring Tool

Coaching Effectiveness Observational Instrument on page 177.

Procedure

1. With one other person from your class, select any children's organized sport experience that you can both observe.

2. The classification system in this study is a simplified version of the CBAS inventory and is taken from Spink (1983). Before observing a coaching session, practice for a minimum of 30 minutes with the Coaching Effectiveness Observational Instrument.

3. Attend one practice session. From a position on the ground that allows both of you to see and hear the coach clearly (and without being obtrusive), observe the practice session for 30 minutes. In this time identify three players who are highly skilled and three players who exhibit poor skills. Designate the former group as skilled athletes and the latter group as unskilled athletes. Be sure that you both agree on the classification of skilled and unskilled athletes.

4. For the next 45 minutes, you and your partner should observe the practice session and independently record all the reinforcements that the skilled and unskilled athletes receive. Use the Coaching Effectiveness Observational Instrument for this purpose. Be sure to note carefully all interactions of the coach toward these athletes and classify them as accurately as possible.

Analysis of Results

1. Total the behavior for each category.
2. Compare your totals with those of your partner who observed the same session.
3. Calculate the following ratios for both skilled and unskilled players:

    Number of positive (praise) reinforcements /
    Number of negative (criticism) reinforcements

    Number of instructions / Total number of reinforcements

    Number of nonreinforcements / Total number of reinforcements

Discussion Questions

1. How similar are your results to those of the other observer? Was there a marked difference in observed behavior? If there were large discrepancies in totals, can you explain the difference? How should you view this data?

2. Did the feedback the coach provided differ for skilled and unskilled athletes? Which categories differed most? Least? Why do you think any differences occurred?

3. What effect might these differences have on the athlete's behavior?

4. How might a coach use this information to improve his or her coaching effectiveness?

References

Barrow, J.C. (1977). The variables of leadership: A review and conceptual framework. *Academy of Management & Review, 2,* 231-251.

Chelladurai, P. (1993). Leadership. In R.N. Singer, M. Murphey, & L.K. Tennant (Eds.), *Handbook of research on sport psychology* (pp. 647-671). New York: Macmillan.

Chelladurai, P., & Saleh, S. (1980). Dimensions of leader behavior in sports: Development of a leadership scale. *Journal of Sport Psychology, 2,* 34-45.

Horn, T.S. (1984). Expectancy effects in the interscholastic athletic setting: Methodological considerations. *Journal of Sport Psychology, 6,* 60-76.

Reimer, H.A., & Chelladurai, P. (1995). Leadership and satisfaction in athletics. *Journal of Sport & Exercise Psychology, 17,* 276-293.

Rosenthal, R., & Jacobson, L. (1968). *Pygmalion in the classroom.* New York: Holt, Rinehart & Winston.

Smoll, F.L., & Smith, R.E. (1989). Leadership behaviors in sport: A theoretical model and research paradigm. *Journal of Applied Social Psychology, 19,* 1522-1551.

Spink, K.S. (1983). Aspects of psychological preparation for the athlete. *Sports Coach, 7,* 24-26, 31-33.

Spink, K.S., & Twardochleb, T. (1996). Modifying the Leadership Scale for Sports for an exercise setting (abstract). *Journal of Sport & Exercise Psychology, 18,* (Suppl.), 78.

Weiss, M.R., & Friedrichs, W. (1986). The influence of leader behaviors, coach attributes, and institutional variables on performance and satisfaction of collegiate basketball teams. *Journal of Sport Psychology, 8,* 332-346.

Coaching Effectiveness Observational Instrument

Category of feedback	Tally each occurrence*	Total	
		Skilled athletes	Unskilled athletes
Praise			
Verbal (e.g., compliments)			
Nonverbal (e.g., smiles)			
Criticism			
Verbal (e.g., insults)			
Nonverbal (e.g., shrugs)			
Instruction			
Verbal (e.g., how-to explanations)			
Nonverbal (e.g., demonstrations)			
Nonreinforcement			

*To facilitate the coding procedure, use an X for feedback to skilled athletes and a check (✔) for feedback to unskilled athletes.

EXPERIENCE 20

EXERCISE ADHERENCE

Everyone is becoming involved in physical fitness. Indeed, over the past few years, television programs dealing with exercise have increased phenomenally, and even actresses are writing best-selling exercise books. All you have to do is visit any bookstore and you are struck by the many books and videos on how to firm this and that part of the anatomy! However, if exercise is good for you, and we all know this, why do so many drop out of exercise programs? The statistics show that more than 50% of adults who start exercise drop out within 6 months (Dishman, 1988). How can they be kept participating for as long as possible?

Objectives

In this learning experience you will learn

- characteristics that have identified potential exercise-program dropouts,
- an alternative approach explaining motivation to engage in or drop out of exercise programs, and
- the sources of information people use to determine whether they will continue or discontinue an exercise program.

Then you will have the opportunity to learn about a new conceptual approach to motivation in exercise and use a qualitative procedure to understand the motivation of individuals to exercise or not to exercise.

Basic Considerations

In recent years, research conducted by exercise physiologists and physicians has established a strong relationship between sedentary lifestyles and an increased risk of developing cardiovascular and cardiorespiratory disease (Dishman, 1988; Falls, Baylor, & Dishman, 1980). As a result, many organized fitness and exercise programs emerged with the objective of reducing the number of inactive individuals within the adult population. The physiological and psychological benefits gained from being involved in habitual physical activity programs have been well documented. However, fitness programs consistently report that only 40% to 65% of the individuals who begin in a program persist in that exercise program. Evidence shows that most individuals drop out at the beginning, with the dropout curve plateauing during the next 10 to 12 months (Dishman, 1982).

Several descriptive studies have investigated situational factors associated with exercise adherence patterns. The accessibility of the exercise setting is an important influence on an individual's exercise involvement. Individuals who reside close to exercise facilities are more likely to stay with the program (Teraslinna, Partanen, Koskela, Partanen, & Oja, 1969). Attitudes of relatives and friends can also influence adherence patterns (Dishman, 1984). The more positive the attitude of these significant others, the better the chances are that a person will remain in the program. However, individuals' attitudes toward exercise and their beliefs about the consequences of behavior practices related to health have not been found to predict adherence (Dishman & Gettman, 1980). Many reasons have been given for not exercising, reasons such as lack of time, lack of knowledge about fitness and how to start properly, lack of facilities, and feeling so fatigued that at the end of the day people are too tired to exercise. Whatever the reason, it is clear that one overarching factor behind not exercising is a lack of motivation.

A promising avenue investigating exercise adherence has been to look at motivation issues. Dishman, Ickes, and Morgan (1980), for example, developed a self-motivation scale based on the premise that some individuals do not have enough self-motivation to adhere to an exercise program. This trait approach to motivation has accurately predicted dropout behavior, but only when self-motivation scores were combined with body-composition measures. Individuals who were likely to drop out were heavier, had higher percentages of body fat, and scored lower on the self-motivation scale than individuals who stayed with the exercise program. The self-motivation scale, combined with body composition measures, is useful in predicting likely dropouts. Once these potential dropouts are identified, however, intervention strategies may be initiated to encourage exercise adherence. However, the motivation component in these studies is not useful in itself. A far more useful avenue has come from the social-cognitive perspective.

An alternative theoretical approach, which considers both situational and personal factors and their interactions, is the *self-efficacy* approach to motivation and persistence in exercise programs (e.g., McAuley, 1992). Sometimes called self-confidence (Feltz, 1992; Gould & Weinberg, 1995), self-efficacy is the perception that one can perform at a certain level on a task, whether that task is an exercise or sport task, or some other task. That perception is assumed to have motivational implications, in that if a person believes he or she has the necessary competencies for the task, and believes he or she can perform at a certain level, then motivation is high to perform the task. If an individual believes he or she does not have the necessary ability, or does not believe he or she can perform at the necessary level, then motivation is low. Many sources of information influence one's level of self-efficacy. These are past performance accomplishments, because what you have done in the past is an important determinant of what you expect to do in the future. Vicarious experiences, or modeling, are important in forming your self-confidence, in that comparison with the experiences of others may influence your behavior. You can convince yourself to complete a task through verbal persuasion, self-talk, or other cognitive procedures that emanate from yourself or significant others. You also can interpret physiological states as indicative of self-efficacy or inefficacy (McAuley, 1992). Thus, there are many sources of self-efficacy expectations.

In the exercise domain, where self-efficacy is popular as a motivational variable, self-efficacy theory states that highly efficacious people are more likely to engage in or adopt desirable activity patterns of exercise. Research has shown that self-efficacy plays a role in exercise participants adhering to exercise programs. In the words of McAuley (1992), "self efficacy mediates exercise behavior" (p. 112). The research supports the role of self-efficacy in individuals adopting and persisting in exercise programs. Although the role is modest, it is consistent enough to be considered an important component in encouraging people to engage in healthy lifestyles such as an exercise program (McAuley, 1992).

If self-efficacy is so important in determining our exercise behavior (or behavior in any context), then it becomes important to enhance self-efficacy if we can. In that way we can facilitate healthy lifestyles. There have been many studies that have tried to enhance self-efficacy. They have all used the various sources we have identified. Research using previous performance to enhance self-efficacy has been successful (see Feltz, 1992). Also, research using vicarious efficacy information and self-persuasive arguments has shown that self-efficacy can be facilitated (Feltz, 1992; McAuley, 1992). However, research with emotional or physiological arousal is equivocal (Feltz, 1992). Other research has shown that positive reinforcement and social support can have a positive influence on self-efficacy (McAuley, 1992). Therefore, we may state that enhancing self-efficacy is possible and desirable within the exercise field. Many people drop out or don't even start because they feel inadequate or incompetent within the physical activity setting. It is important for people to feel comfortable and to have the necessary competencies to engage in the task successfully. To promote exercise, it is necessary to enhance self-efficacy.

With the rising concern about maintaining healthy lifestyles, adherence has assumed importance in the exercise field. Once upon a time, it was considered sufficient to educate people about the consequences of not exercising! However, as with the antismoking campaigns, knowledge that certain lifestyles are good or bad is not enough. To adopt and maintain healthy lifestyles is a matter of motivation as much as knowledge that if you do not change, dire consequences may follow. Therefore, to understand people who are trying to change their lifestyle, knowing their perception of their ability to execute the behaviors necessary is crucial. Thus, this learning experience in exercise adherence gives you the opportunity to collect data on self-efficacy, using a qualitative approach to understanding the motivation of people who are engaging in and contemplating beginning an exercise program.

Learning Experience

Purpose

To interview individuals about their perceptions of engaging in an exercise program.

Measuring Tool

There is no exercise adherence data sheet. What you do in this experience is interview two people, then categorize their responses as to the sources of their self-efficacy.

Procedure

1. Select two individuals. One is a person actively engaging in an exercise program (not a training program for a sport but an exercise program to maintain health or physique). Activities such as running or swimming, at least 3 times a week, for 30 minutes per day would qualify as an acceptable activity. The second individual is a person who wants to exercise, but who starts and drops out, or just never gets around to it. This is a person who knows he or she should exercise, but finds getting started and maintaining the regimen is difficult.

2. Interview both people about their reasons for exercising, and ask them why they want to exercise. Then ask them about the difficulty of exercising—do they find it easy or difficult; do they believe they can maintain the activity, and so on (see the following list of suggested questions).

3. Have each person answer the following questions, but these are only suggestions. You can ask questions to get at the issues you wish in this context; just remember you are investigating the person's motivation to exercise. A good technique is to record the responses of each participant so you can go over them in your own time. Also, it allows the conversation to flow.

4. Here are some suggested questions. However, you must follow where the participant leads and ask follow-up questions to find the motivational determinants of the interviewee.

 1. Do you enjoy exercising?
 2. Why do you enjoy (not enjoy) exercising?
 3. Do you feel that you can do the activity OK?
 4. Are you confident you can exercise 3 times a week for at least 30 minutes? Why or why not?
 5. How do you feel when you contemplate going out to exercise?
 6. Just before you exercise, how do you feel?
 7. Why do you exercise?
 8. What is it that makes you feel you want to exercise (not want to exercise)?

Analysis of Results

1. Use content analysis to determine the responses of each participant. Look to page 25 at the content analysis procedure approach.
2. Look carefully at the responses. What does the participant say about the

motivation to do (or not do) the exercise? Can you detect self-efficacy variables in the responses? From a self-efficacy perspective, do the responses reveal the person's motivation and his or her reasons for doing or not doing the exercise?

Discussion Questions

1. Did you find self-efficacy thinking in the responses of the individuals?
2. Could the reasons be described by self-efficacy?
3. What implications do these results have for intervention strategies?
4. Were there differences between the exerciser and the nonexerciser?

References

Dishman, R.K. (1982). Compliance/adherence in health-related exercise. *Health Psychology, 1,* 237-267.

Dishman, R.K. (1984). Motivation and exercise adherence. In J. Silva & R. Weinberg (Eds.), *Psychological foundations of sport and exercise* (pp. 420-434). Champaign, IL: Human Kinetics.

Dishman, R.K. (1988). *Exercise adherence: Its impact on public health.* Champaign, IL: Human Kinetics.

Dishman, R.K., & Gettman, L.R. (1980). Psychobiological influences in exercise adherence. *Journal of Sport Psychology, 2,* 295-310.

Dishman, R.K., Ickes, W.J., & Morgan, W.P. (1980). Self-motivation and adherence to therapeutic exercise. *Journal of Applied Social Psychology, 10,* 115-131.

Falls, H.B., Baylor, A.M., & Dishman, R.K. (1980). *Essentials of fitness.* Philadelphia: Saunders College/Holt, Rinehart & Winston.

Feltz, D.L. (1992). Motivation in sport: A self-efficacy perspective. In G.C. Roberts (Ed.), *Motivation in sport and exercise* (pp. 93-106). Champaign, IL: Human Kinetics.

Gould, D. & Weinberg, R. (1995). *Foundations of sport and exercise psychology.* Champaign, IL: Human Kinetics.

McAuley, E. (1992). Understanding exercise behavior. In G.C. Roberts (Ed.), *Motivation in sport and exercise* (pp. 107-128). Champaign, IL: Human Kinetics.

Teraslinna, P., Partanen, T., Koskela, A., Partanen, K., & Oja, P. (1969). Characteristics affecting willingness of executives to participate in an activity program aimed at coronary heart disease prevention. *Journal of Sports Medicine and Physical Fitness, 9,* 224-229.

INDEX

ABOUT THE AUTHORS

Glyn C. Roberts, PhD, is a professor of sport psychology at the Norwegian University of Sport Science. He was a member of the Department of Kinesiology from 1973 to 1998 at the University of Illinois, Urbana-Champaign, where he is now professor emeritus. Dr. Roberts' research has focused on the motivational determinants of achievement and children in the competitive sport experience. He is regarded as one of the leading authorities in the world on motivation and achievement in the sport experience, especially for children.

The author of more than 100 publications, Dr. Roberts has written or edited 14 books, as well as 36 book chapters. He has made more than 250 presentations, including more than 30 keynote addresses at international congresses. In 1998 he was named as a Distinguished Scholar of the North American Society for the Psychology of Sport and Physical Activity (NASPSPA), only one of six people so recognized by NASPSPA.

Kevin S. Spink, **PhD,** is a professor of sport psychology in the College of Kinesiology at the University of Saskatchewan. He is the author or co-author of five previous books on sport psychology and is a former Associate Editor of the *Journal of Applied Sport Psychology*. Dr. Spink has been widely published in journals of sport and exercise psychology and has lectured on the subject internationally.

Dr. Spink is a member of the Association for the Advancement of Applied Sport Psychology (AAASP), NASPSPA, and the International Association of Applied Psychology. He also is a member of the Board of Directors for the Canadian Fitness and Lifestyle Research Institute.

Cynthia Pemberton, PhD, is an Associate Professor at the University of Missouri-Kansas City, where she is the chairperson of the Department of Physical Education. She received her PhD in sport and exercise psychology from the University of Illinois at Urbana-Champaign.

Dr. Pemberton is a Certified Consultant in AAASP and a member of the United States Olympic Committee Sport Psychology Registry. She is also a Fellow in the Research Consortium of the American Alliance for Health, Physical Education, Recreation and Dance and has served as a Past President of the American Association for Active Lifestyles and Fitness.

RELATED BOOKS FROM HUMAN KINETICS

Foundations of Sport and Exercise Psychology
Robert S. Weinberg, PhD, and Daniel Gould, PhD
1995 • Hardcover • 544 pp • Item BWEI0812
ISBN 0-87322-812-X • $52.00 ($77.95 Cdn)
Uses visuals and anecdotes, case studies, and stories from the world of sport and exercise to explain key concepts in the field and show how they apply to counseling, teaching, coaching, and fitness instruction.

Instructor Guide for Foundations of Sport and Exercise Psychology
Daniel Gould, PhD, and Robert S. Weinberg, PhD
1995 • 3 1/2" disk • Windows and Macintosh software available • **FREE** to course adopters of *Foundations of Sport and Exercise Psychology*
Uses a point-and-click format to search for questions from the test bank, create original questions, and edit and print in test form. Includes the TestStats Manager, a test record module that allows the professor to record and print a gradebook containing test scores. Automatically computes statistics for the entered test scores.

Embracing Your Potential
Terry Orlick, PhD
1998 • Paper • 208 pp • Item PORL0831 • ISBN 0-88011-831-8 $15.95 ($22.95 Cdn)
Explains how to achieve excellence and balance in both the public/performance and personal/experiential domains of life. Addresses "Gold" and "Green" zones. The Gold Zone includes visible, tangible achievement markers, such as performance results, career advancement, win-loss records, and financial status. The Green Zone involves relationships and intellectual, spiritual, cultural, and joyful recreational pursuits.

To request more information or to order, U.S. customers call 1-800-747-4457, e-mail us at **humank@hkusa.com**, or visit our Web site at **http://www.humankinetics.com/**. Persons outside the U.S. can contact us via our Web site or use the appropriate telephone number, postal address, or e-mail address shown in the front of this book.

HUMAN KINETICS
The Information Leader in Physical Activity